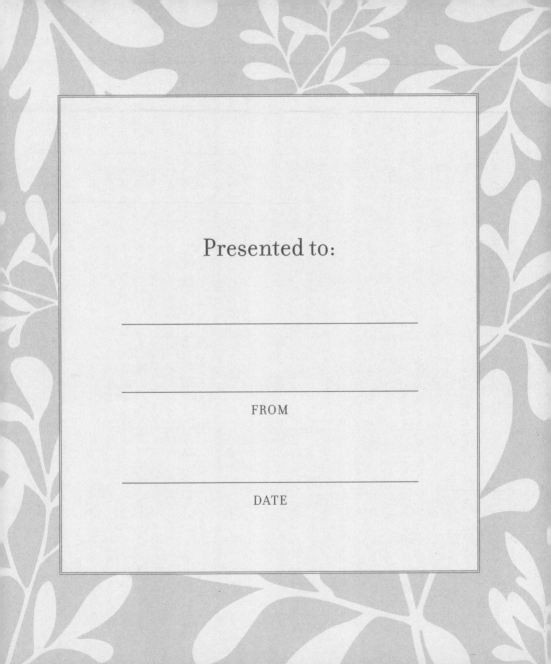

Presented to:

_____

_____
FROM

_____
DATE

the Art of Encouragement

A SIMPLE GUIDE TO LIVING LIFE FROM THE HEART

Candy Paull

Stewart, Tabori & Chang

New York

Editor: Marisa Bulzone
Designer: LeAnna Weller Smith
Production Manager: Kim Tyner

Library of Congress Cataloging-in-Publication
Data:

Paull, Candy.
The art of encouragement : a simple guide to
living life from the heart / by Candy Paull.
        p. cm.
    ISBN 10: 1-58479-446-1
    ISBN 13: 978-1-58479-446-2
    1. Encouragement. 2. Encouragement--
Quotations, maxims, etc. I. Title.

BJ1475.5.P38 2006
179'.9--dc22

2005029807

Originally published in 2002 by Winding Stair
Press, an imprint of Stewart House Publishing
Inc., Toronto, Canada.

Published in 2006 by
Stewart, Tabori & Chang
An imprint of
Harry N. Abrams, Inc.

The text of this book was composed in Corporate S,
Filosofia and Type Embellishments.

Printed in China by Midas Printing Co., Ltd.

10 9 8 7 6 5 4 3 2

HNA ■■■■■
harry n. abrams, inc.
a subsidiary of La Martinière Groupe

115 West 18th Street
New York, NY 10011
www.hnabooks.com

To all the teachers, mentors, colleagues, co-writers, and friends who have encouraged me over the years, and to my mother, Ruth Paull, who helped me bring this project to fruition.

contents

INTRODUCTION

Encouragement is the art of abundance shared and multiplied. It is a way of living that seeks to bless every person we meet. Encouragement looks at what we can be, believes in the best in each of us. Encouragement is love in action. It is taking time to appreciate everyone we meet.

When the world and all its pressures take the heart out of us, we need to know that someone cares for and believes in us. And we need to do the same for others. Encouragement means taking time to let God encourage us, to meditate on the small miracles of life. Enthusiasm and courage, love and appreciation, practical acts of mercy and compassion—that's the way of encouragement. The art of encouragement is the art of creating community and celebrating friendship.

In my first book, *The Art of Abundance*, I talked about counting your blessings. Now I'm encouraging you to *be* a blessing. I encourage you to make a circle of giving. Dare to dream for yourself, for one another, for your community, and for our world. *The Art of Encouragement* offers a collection of quotes, meditations, and ideas for encouraging ourselves, encouraging others, and making a difference in our own corner of the world. It is my prayer that this little book will enable you to say yes to the deepest promptings of your heart and to create a life that nurtures your soul.

Candy Paull

Encouragement Is Love in Action

You will find as you look back upon your life that the moments when you have really lived are the moments when you have done things in a spirit of love.

—HENRY DRUMMOND

Encouragement is . . . inspiring each other to embrace life with enthusiasm, courage, and love.

Encouragement is . . . a warm shoulder in a cold world.

Encouragement is . . . a cup of tea and a listening ear.

Encouragement is . . . being loved for who you are.

Friendship is the only cement that will ever hold the world together.
—WOODROW WILSON

Nothing is so contagious as enthusiasm;
it moves stones, it charms brutes.
Enthusiasm is the genius of sincerity,
and truth accomplishes no victories without it.
—EDWARD BULWER-LYTTON

In every moment of genuine love,
we are dwelling in God and God in us.
—PAUL TILLICH

Encouragement is . . . seeing the unique beauty in another person.

Encouragement is . . . saying "I love you."

Encouragement is . . . a card sent not for a special occasion,
but just "because."

There is nothing on this earth more to be prized
than true friendship.
—SAINT THOMAS AQUINAS

VISION

Where there is no vision, the people perish.
—PROVERBS 29:18 (KJV)

R eal encouragement that makes a lasting difference is visionary. It is the willingness to imagine a good future, the choice to believe in a better world. It is not critical, tearing people down and nitpicking at their faults, but instead valuing their uniqueness and seeing potential that they may not be able to see for themselves. In many ways, a true encourager functions as a personal prophet, helping others discover their own potential and make it incarnate in the physical world.

Real encouragement sees us as we yearn to be seen, sees others as they long to be seen, and the world as it is meant to be seen. Yes, there are faults, problems, evil—but there is an original vision that our deepest hearts know is the true vision. Real encouragers are willing to be fools in the eyes of cynics because they have a great vision, like Martin Luther King, Jr., who dared to say to a country, "I have a dream . . ."

Each friend represents a world in us,
a world possibly not born until they arrive,
and it is only by this meeting
that a new world is born.

—ANAÏS NIN

Follow the grain in your own wood.

—HOWARD THURMAN

Self-conquest is really self-surrender.
Yet before we can surrender ourselves we must become ourselves.
For no one can give up what he does not possess.

—THOMAS MERTON

W hen we learn the art of encouragement, we learn to see the good in ourselves, as well as in others. Before we can give to others, we must have something to give. We become like gardeners who look at bare soil and see the flowers and fruit that could grow there. Or we become like architects who envision a beautiful building on an empty lot. A gardener sees what the garden can be and then takes practical steps to plant, weed, cultivate, water, wait, and eventually reap a good harvest. An architect imagines what a building can be, examines the site, draws up the plans, and works with the construction team and the new owners to create a place where others will live, work, and play.

Encouragers do not merely set goals but reach for the stars. They dare to dream first, then find ways to make the dream come true. Yet they do not force their patterns or desires on others. Instead they become visionaries who see the unique fingerprint of God in every person and treasure the sacredness of each human being, including themselves.

What do you dare to dream for yourself?
What do you dare to dream for others?
What do you dare to dream for your community?
What do you dare to dream for our world?

I don't know what your destiny will be,
but one thing I know: the only ones among you
who will be really happy
are those who have sought and found how to serve.
—ALBERT SCHWEITZER

Mankind's role is to fulfill his heaven-sent purpose
through a sincere heart that is in harmony
with all creation and loves all things.
—MORIHEI USEHIBA

LOVE IN ACTION

I am a little pencil in the hand of a writing God
who is sending a love letter to the world.
—MOTHER TERESA

This seeing and encouraging of potential in people and circumstances can't just remain a neat, pretty vision in the mind. It needs to be acted out, incarnated (fleshed out, made real) in this physical world where we live, move, and have our being. Small specific acts of encouragement help us move from our heads and hearts to our hands and feet.

Here are some simple ideas that make love visible and physical:

❖ Take time to share a nurturing meal.

❖ Write cards and letters.

❖ When you are thinking of someone, pick up the phone and call.

❖ Say it with flowers.

- Give little gifts that say "I'm thinking of you," even when there is no special occasion.
- Share back rubs, hugs, touching, cuddling.
- Smile.
- Say a few kind words.
- Welcome others into your home.
- Organize your closet and give clothes you never wear to someone who can use them.
- Offer to drive someone to a doctor's appointment.
- Love a pet.
- Plant some seeds and grow a garden.
- Make a big pot of soup and share it.
- Take time to listen to a friend.
- Volunteer.
- Say thank you.

No one is useless in this world who lightens the burdens of another.
—CHARLES DICKENS

Helping others, that's the main thing.
The only way for us to help ourselves is to help others
and to listen to each other's stories.
—ELI WIESEL

Love bears all things, believes all things, hopes all things, endures all things.
—I CORINTHIANS 13:7 (RSV)

The capacity to be of service to the greater good
requires that we have the security to risk our image,
our position, and our pride in the search for greater justice—
at the workplace, in our families, and in our community at large.
—MARK BRYAN, JULIA CAMERON, AND CATHERINE ALLEN

If civilization is to survive, we must cultivate the science
of human relationships—the ability of all peoples,
of all kinds, to live together, in the same world at peace.
—FRANKLIN DELANO ROOSEVELT

Alone we can do so little; together we can do so much.
—HELEN KELLER

We know God wipes away all tears,
but it certainly feels good when
He uses human hands.
—MARY PAULSON-LAUDA

Every man rejoices twice when he has a partner in his joy. He who
shares tears with us wipes them away. He divides them in two, and
he who laughs with us makes the joy double.
—BISHOP FULTON J. SHEEN

Bear one another's burdens . . .

—GALATIANS 6:2 (RSV)

To love deeply in one direction makes us more loving in all others.

—MADAME SWETCHINE

Do not think that love, in order to be genuine,
has to be extraordinary.
What we need is to love without getting tired.

—MOTHER TERESA

How rich you are is measured by how many true friends you have.

—HAMZA EL DIN

Everything in life responds to the song of the heart.

—ERNEST HOLMES

THE OPTIMIST'S CHOICE

The accumulation of small, optimistic acts
produces quality in our culture and in your life.
Our culture resonates in tense times to individual acts of grace.

—JENNIFER JAMES

Encouragement means believing in the best in situations and believing the best of people. It is not encouraging to dwell on the negatives. Energy expands when we think positively and contracts when we dwell on negative thoughts. To make the optimist's choice is not to be an ostrich, burying your head in the sand and pretending problems don't exist. Optimism is an attitude that believes we can make a positive difference with our choices, no matter how small the act, no matter how large the problem.

This optimism has its feet firmly planted on a foundation of faith in a benign universe guided by a Higher Power, a God who brings healing and transformation through our positive choices and attitudes. Science is finding that we can actually create a positive energy feedback loop—or a negative one—just by focusing our intentions and then acting on our beliefs. As a photographer chooses to focus on particular elements of a landscape, so we can choose to focus on the possibilities in the landscape of our lives.

We shall never know all the good
that a simple smile can do.
—MOTHER TERESA

Some Taoists practice the "inner smile," which relaxes and revitalizes the body, enabling the spirit to lighten its load of heavy problems. Unlike a grumpy, indifferent, or resentful attitude, a smiling attitude can put us at ease and transform a situation. Think of statues of the Buddha that you have seen—calm and serene, detached, yet smiling. When you are disturbed by a person, a thing, or an event, visualize yourself smiling as calmly as that benign Buddha. Look at the person, thing, or event. Allow the goodness and energy of life to enfold and envelop you and the person or problem you are facing. Feel the tension dissipate; let your tight muscles relax. Let go of your expectations and judgments. Breathe peace in. Breathe resistance out. Relax and allow the healing power of love to enter your soul. Can you feel your defensiveness and fear melting away?

I have found this to be a good exercise when I wake up in the middle of the night and start worrying a problem like a dog worrying a bone. It is easy to go round and round in a squirrely circle, brooding over the problem or hurt or worry and getting nowhere. But if I smile in the dark and create an opening for positive energy to enter, it is like pulling focus away from the problem and opening the eye to see the wider and more timeless context. As a smile can literally relax and lighten a tight face (it takes fewer muscles to smile than to frown), so an inner smile can help relax a tight mind. It is a small way in which to make the optimist's choice. If we choose to resonate to positive attitudes and believe for the best, the world is able to resonate with us and tune us into a melody of forgiveness, harmony, and childlike trust.

Five minutes, just before going to sleep,
given to a bit of directed imagination regarding
achievement possibilities of the morrow,
will steadily and increasingly bear fruit,
particularly if all ideas of difficulty,
worry, or fear are resolutely ruled out and replaced
by those of accomplishment and smiling courage.

—FREDERICK PIERCE

The first rule is to keep an untroubled spirit.
The second is to look things in the face and know them for what they are.
—MARCUS AURELIUS

Do not struggle. Go with the flow of things, and you will find yourself at one
with the mysterious unity of the universe.
—CHUANG TZU

As your faith is strengthened you will find that there is
no longer the need to have a sense of control, that things will flow as they will,
and that you will flow with them, to your great delight and benefit.
—EMMANUEL TENEY

Every morning I spend fifteen minutes filling my mind full of God,
and so there's no room left for worry thoughts.
—HOWARD CHANDLER CHRISTY

The best doctors in the world are Doctor Diet, Doctor Quiet, and Doctor Merryman.
—JONATHAN SWIFT

Worry affects the circulation, the heart, the glands, the whole nervous system, and profoundly affects the health. You have never known a man who died from overwork, but many who died from doubt. . . . Half the beds in our hospitals are filled with people who worried themselves into them.

—DR. CHARLES MAYO

Heavy thoughts bring on physical maladies;
when the soul is oppressed, so is the body.

—MARTIN LUTHER

Worry often gives a small thing a big shadow.

—SWEDISH PROVERB

A cheerful heart is a good medicine,
but a downcast spirit dries up the bones.

—PROVERBS 17:22 (RSV)

For every minute you are angry, you lose sixty seconds of happiness.

—RALPH WALDO EMERSON

Calmness is power.

—JAMES ALLEN

Energy is bliss.

—WILLIAM BLAKE

Some things have to be believed to be seen.

—RALPH HODGSON

For we walk by faith, not by sight.

—II CORINTHIANS 5:7 (RSV)

Doubt is a pain too lonely to know
that faith is his twin brother.

—KAHLIL GIBRAN

Believe that life is worth living,
and your belief will help create that fact.

—WILLIAM JAMES

28

All effort is in the last analysis sustained by faith
that it is worth making.

—ORDWAY TWEED

A cheerful frame of mind, reinforced by relaxation,
which in itself banishes fatigue,
is the medicine that puts all ghosts of fear on the run.

—GEORGE MATTHEW ADAMS

The only limit to our realization of tomorrow will be our doubts of today.
Let us move forward with strong and active faith.

—FRANKLIN DELANO ROOSEVELT

Therefore do not be anxious about tomorrow,
for tomorrow will be anxious for itself.

—MATTHEW 6:34 (RSV)

A day of worrying is more exhausting than a day of work.

—JOHN LUBBOCK

The Art of Encouragement

Our minds can shape the way a thing will be
because we act according to our expectations.
—FEDERICO FELLINI

You can't depend on your eyes
when your imagination is out of focus.
—MARK TWAIN

We fear our highest possibility (as well as our lowest one).
We are generally afraid to become
that which we can glimpse in our most perfect moments.
—ABRAHAM MASLOW

Man can only receive what he sees himself receiving.
—FLORENCE SCOVEL SHINN

Too many people are thinking of security instead of opportunity.
They are more afraid of life than death.
—JAMES F. BYRNES

Dream lofty dreams, and as you dream, so shall you become.
Your vision is the promise of what you shall at last unveil.
—JOHN RUSKIN

The life each of us lives is the life within the limits of our own thinking. To have
life more abundant, we must think in limitless terms of abundance.
—THOMAS DREIER

Love is available to me in many forms.
Today I will broaden my rigid notions of how love is to
be packaged and delivered. I will open myself to receiving
the vast expressions of God's love in this world.
—ROKELLE LERNER

You must keep chasing that dream. Don't give up.
It won't be easy, but don't give up.
Shoot for the stars. Maybe you won't make it as high as you hoped, but more
than likely you'll land someplace along the way. Fill your heart with as much
love as you can, and don't hold it in. Share it with everybody you can.
—CARL PERKINS

31

All Times are His Seasons

We ask our daily bread, and God never says, You should have come yesterday. He never says, You must come again tomorrow. But "today if you will hear His voice," today He will hear you. If some king of the earth have so large an extent of dominion in north and south as that he hath winter and summer together in his dominions, so large an extent of east and west as that he hath day and night together in his dominions, much more hath God mercy and judgement together. He brought light out of darkness, not out of a lesser light. He can bring thy summer out of winter though thou have no spring. Though in the ways of fortune, or misunderstanding, or conscience, thou have been benighted till now, wintered and frozen, clouded and eclipsed, damp and benumbed, smothered and stupefied till now, now God comes to thee, not as in the dawning of the day, not as in the bud of the spring, but as the sun at noon, to banish all shadows; as the sheaves in harvest, to fill all penuries. All occasions invite His mercies, and all times are His seasons.

God made the sun and moon to distinguish seasons, and day and night; and we cannot have the fruits of earth but in their seasons. But God hath made no decrees to distinguish the seasons of His mercies. In Paradise the fruits were ripe the first minute, and in Heaven it is always autumn. His mercies are ever in their maturity.

—JOHN DONNE

Learning to Love Without Fear

When you look at the world in a narrow way, how narrow it seems!

When you look at it in a mean way, how mean it is!

When you look at it selfishly, how selfish it is!

But when you look at it in a broad, generous, friendly spirit,

what wonderful people you find in it.

—HORACE RUTLEDGE

CHOOSE LOVE OVER FEAR

There is no fear in love . . .
—I JOHN 4:18 (RSV)

*By consistently choosing love rather than fear, we can experience
a personal transformation that enables us to be more naturally loving to
ourselves and others. In this way we can begin to recognize and
experience the love and joy that unites us.*
—DR. JERRY JAMPOLSKY

W e have the choice. We can choose to live in fear or we can choose to live in love. Encouragement is about believing the best—of ourselves, of others, of life. Fear is a choice to believe the worst. Frequently, the most encouraging option comes out of love and choosing to believe that a benign universe will respond to our attitude of faith. To believe for the best is to choose to believe that God is good and that what He does is good. It is to believe that there is a Higher Power that responds to our positive attitudes and actions. This is not to discount the pain, sorrow, and disappointment that come with life. But we can choose to move beyond a limiting and fearful view of how life works and learn to practice the kind of optimism that opens the doors of opportunity, change, and blessing.

Optimism is a choice that changes your trajectory. I have found that if you fear the worst, you create what you expect. You make choices out of fear and limit your options. But what would happen if you made choices on the assumption that things would work out? What would life be like if you decided that God was truly interested in helping you, and that difficult people and situations were heaven-sent lessons that could lead to greater personal growth and a better life? Would you like to have the kind of faith that chooses love over fear?

I have found that practical optimism helps grease the wheels of life, releasing energy for growth and change. I have wasted too much energy on fearing what could happen (which never did happen). When really tough things have come along in my life—the things I most dreaded—I discovered that I was cared for and led along step by step. Even when I was facing the death of a loved one, I found that the great loss was tempered by hope, faith, and the love of others who shared my loss. Most of the imagined fears that once drained my energy now seem small and meaningless in light of the larger issues of life. So now I have become more daring, willing to take risks and gamble that love will win over fear every time.

I am constantly being challenged to make the choice between fear and love. I choose love over fear when I focus on doing what I really enjoy and am good at, rather than aiming only for a secure paycheck. (Paychecks can be very false security—they can disappear so fast, and I could be out of a job with a corporate buyout or a change in the marketplace.) I choose love when I face my fears and go for my dreams anyway. I choose love when I reach out to someone else. I choose love when I trust the process, even when I don't have all the answers. Choosing love is an act of courage. We all carry that courage deep inside our hearts.

I have found that if you love life, it will love you back.
—ARTUR RUBINSTEIN

For in reality, none of us know what the future holds.
So we can choose to imagine it either in nihilistic terms (if we do this, all work
stops) or as a playground of possibilities for our species and loved ones
(if we do this, creativity can begin anew . . .).
—MATTHEW FOX

Where there is great love, there are always miracles.
—WILLA CATHER

. . . perfect love casts out fear.
—I JOHN 4:18 (RSV)

Each of us makes our own weather, determines the color of the skies in the emotional universe which he inhabits.
—BISHOP FULTON J. SHEEN

Fear believes . . . there is never enough.
Love believes . . . there is plenty for everyone.

Fear believes . . . the worst about people and situations.
Love believes . . . the best about people and situations.

Fear believes . . . there is only one right answer.
Love believes . . . there are many ways to understand something.

Fear believes . . . you have to change others through
manipulation and coercion to get what you want.
Love believes . . . real change comes from the heart,
starting with your own heart.

As the hand is made for holding and the eye for seeing,
Thou hast fashioned me for joy.
Share with me the vision that shall find it everywhere.
—GAELIC PRAYER

Fear believes . . . things will never change.
Love believes . . . any situation can be transformed by the power of love.

Fear believes . . . that everything must be mapped out ahead of time.
Love believes . . . that you can trust the process.

Fear believes . . . in negative thinking.
Love believes . . . in positive choice.

Fear believes . . . the damage is done.
Love believes . . . healing can happen.

The night is the mother of the day
The winter of the spring
And even upon old decay
The greenest mosses cling.
—JOHN GREENLEAF WHITTIER

Fear believes . . . if you're not a success by now, you must be a failure.
Love believes . . . you're only a failure if you give up on your dreams.

Fear believes . . . I must do everything with my own strength.
Love believes . . . there is a Higher Power that wants to help me.

Fear believes . . . that everything needs to hyped.
Love believes . . . in quiet strength and simple faith.

Fear believes . . . life is cheap.
Love believes . . . life is precious.

O rich and various man! Thou palace of sight and sound,
carrying in thy senses the morning and the night,
and the unfathomable galaxy; in thy heart, the power of love.
—RALPH WALDO EMERSON

Fear believes . . . anyone different is "them."
Love believes . . . there is only "us."

Fear believes . . . it's too late.
Love believes . . . it's never too late.

Fear believes . . . the situation is impossible.
Love believes . . . a solution can be found.

Fear believes . . . that fifteen minutes of fame makes you important.
Love believes . . . we are all important.

We are given appetites, not to consume the world and forget it,
but to taste its goodness and hunger to make it great.

—ROBERT FARRAR CAPON

Fear believes . . . people are disposable commodities.
Love believes . . . people are sacred.

Fear believes . . . in proving your own superiority over others.
Love believes . . . in honoring the greatness in others.

Fear believes . . . no one is listening and no one cares.
Love believes . . . in prayer.

Fear believes . . . effort is only justified by outward success.
Love believes . . . sometimes we need to do something for its own sake.

It is not a matter of thinking much, so do whatever most kindles love in you.

—SAINT TERESA OF AVILA

Hope is like a road in the country;
there was never a road,
but when many people walk on it,
the road comes into existence.

—LIN YUTANG

The art of living lies less in eliminating our troubles
than in growing with them.

—BERNARD M. BARUCH

I'm not happy, I'm cheerful.
There's a difference.
A happy woman has no cares at all.
A cheerful woman has cares but has
learned how to deal with them.

—BEVERLY SILLS

PUTTING THE HEART (AND SPICE) BACK INTO LIFE

Why not go out on a limb? Isn't that where the fruit is?

—FRANK SCULLY

The root of *encouragement* is the French word *coeur*, for heart. To encourage is to put the heart back into someone, to help each other live well and live together. We were created for love and community. Yet we live in a competitive world that discourages us, telling us all the ways we don't measure up and why we need this product or that service to overcome our inadequacies. There is a great emphasis on what we lack—the messages in the media are rooted in fear and manipulation. What we need is the courage to claim our own lives, to have the confidence to live with resolution, vitality, and purpose.

I wish to make the most of what I have and to make a contribution to this world. I am not here to have everything, to own everything, to be, do, or conquer everything. I am here to do some work and then move on. I am here to contribute my bit to humanity, to the stream of time, to each reality that I am part of. If some of my contributions extend beyond my physical life on this earth, that is good and sweet. It is my work to love this earth, to love and be with these people who have come, by divine timing, into my life. It is no accident that I am here, intersecting with these particular people in this particular time and place. It is up to me to make each choice and each encounter the best experience possible by using what I have. As I choose to live my life with courage, I infuse courage into the hearts of others, helping to bring good for each other into being.

I like life with juice and kick. I used to think I was merely a nice girl who must compromise and conform to keep the peace, diminishing myself to fit into a preconceived role. But lately I have discovered in myself a spicy woman who likes diversity and differences. I have learned that I do not have to fit myself into a mold to be popular or powerful, or to gain some worldly advantage. I can accept myself as God created me, not as "inferior" or "superior," but as a human being with faults and foibles, with both limitations and untapped possibilities.

I have redefined who I am and how I see myself. Now I know that I am an artist, a musician, and a writer—a creative person with gifts to share. I am a student of life, a romantic, a friend, an individual who is a mystery to explore and who is learning how to love. As I have learned to name the things I love, I have found that I no longer have to keep proving myself or defining myself by a set of standards that measure the wrong things. As I learn my craft as an artist, the materials themselves teach me about who I am and what I am made of. As I learn to love others, I learn something new about the love of God.

It takes courage to move from the illusion of safety and easy answers into the unexplored territory of questions and new ideas. In recent years, I have moved away from a formal interpretation of religious belief toward a more open approach to my relationship with the God who created the universe. True freedom comes with accepting that I don't have all the answers and that life is guaranteed to surprise me. God does not have to fit into my neat little boxes any more. I no longer need to pigeonhole or judge. I don't have to be so hard on myself—or on others.

I used to be so worried about what others thought. Others *are* thinking—but not about me. I had a million scenarios playing in my mind, created by a judgmental inner censor telling me everything that I was doing wrong. I would project that censor's attitude onto others, assuming that they must be judging me as narrowly as I judged myself. And I assumed that God was also busy weighing and measuring me, wanting to "fix" me at every turn. I found it a stifling way to live—I felt restricted by my own fears and judgments.

Our culture and our psychology work on a disease/cure, problem/fix model, so we tend to define ourselves by our diagnoses. We look at everything

47

as a problem to be solved. We want to "fix" everything so it can live up to some artificial standard of perfection. We judge ourselves harshly for being different, call our uniqueness failure, and see our struggles as a collection of symptoms needing diagnosis, prescription, and cure.

What if we decide to see our "shortcomings" in a different light? What if we give ourselves permission to be unique, instead of playing an assigned role that doesn't fit? What if we allow ourselves to honor our true natures, to listen to the goodness and wisdom that reside deep in our hearts?

I am learning to honor my individuality and my own unique viewpoint. I am not a demographic, I am a person. I have learned to listen to the deep wisdom of my heart and my intuition, and I have found it to be truthful at all times. Sometimes I am afraid to say my truth out loud, but my heart knows it, even when my lips and my life deny it. I have been learning to align my choices with my heart's desires, to admit what I really want and to say no to that which no longer belongs in my life. As I am doing this, I am also able to do it for others—to help them name their own truths and honor their highest instincts.

I live in a community of nonconformists. Artists, writers, musicians—we have all come to this community to seek our dreams. And we all felt a bit like misfits back home, not because we weren't loved or because we prided ourselves on being nonconformist rebels, but because we just never felt like we fit in successfully. Our need for a certain kind of creative life called for us to live differently than most people. We were not successes in the rat race—most of us preferred to listen to our friends sing or to make art or music ourselves, rather than to make money or gain prestige and power.

Most regular jobs seemed boring, a means to an end—a way to pay the bills and buy enough time to practice our craft.

"What do you want to do for a living?"

"Write songs."

"Oh."

One could just as well have said "bet on the ponies at the racetrack" for a vocational choice, considering the difficulties and craziness of a professional career in music. Any songwriter who has spent time in the trenches of the music industry knows that trying for a hit song (let alone multiple hits) is a lot like betting on racehorses. This is a choice that does not stack up well against such careers as doctor, lawyer, engineer, or professor, at least in the eyes of concerned family and friends. They wonder how soon it will be before the poor songwriter finally settles down and gets a "real job."

Now I live in a community where creative people of all stripes gather. I have found others who want to "waste" their time doodling with color and noodling with notes and exploring the outer reaches of the creative landscape. In this communion of creatives, our choices are affirmed, our struggles are understood, and we have fellow travelers to walk with down a difficult but fulfilling road.

We have learned to name our deepest truths, accept our limitations, value our callings, and give ourselves permission to be a little more quirky, a little more individualistic. We live our lives from the heart, even if we still have "day jobs" that pay the bills. Some of us have even found a way to make a living doing what we love. It's worth the price we've paid, just to be a part of such a vibrant community. I am surrounded by amazing people who live heartfelt lives of extraordinary courage.

But you don't have to be an artist or a songwriter to value creativity and community. I believe that we are all creative, that we all deserve to be encouraged in our endeavors, and that every person can learn to cultivate his or her own uniqueness. Everyone must eventually choose between sterile conformity and listening to their inner wisdom. Everyone comes to a crossroads where they must decide either to honor their individuality or to stay in the constricting box of cultural expectations. Every person has the potential to find a community of like-minded people and to create a matrix of safety and encouragement for personal and collective growth and creativity.

The question is not what a man can scorn,

or disparage, or find fault with,

but what he can love, and value, and appreciate.

—JOHN RUSKIN

One has to abandon altogether

the search for security,

and reach out to the risk of living with both arms.

One has to embrace the world like a lover.

—MORRIS L. WEST

Keep your fears to yourself,

but share your courage with others.

—ROBERT LOUIS STEVENSON

Salutation of the Dawn

Listen to the Exhortation of the Dawn!
Look to this Day!
For it is Life, the very Life of Life.
In its brief course lie all the
Verities and Realities of your Existence:

    The Bliss of Growth,

    The Glory of Action,

    The Splendor of Beauty,

For Yesterday is but a Dream,
And Tomorrow is only a Vision:
But Today well-lived makes
Every Yesterday a Dream of Happiness,
And every Tomorrow a Vision of Hope.
Look well therefore to this Day!
Such is the Salutation of the Dawn!

—FROM THE SANSKRIT

Follow your bliss.

—JOSEPH CAMPBELL

A man should learn to detect and watch that gleam of light
which flashes across his mind from within,
more than the lustre of the firmament of bards and sages.
Yet he dismisses without notice his thought, because it is his.
In every work of genius we recognize our own rejected thoughts:
they come back to us with a certain alienated majesty.

—RALPH WALDO EMERSON

I do the very best I know how—the very best I can;
and I mean to keep doing so until the end.
If the end brings me out all right, what is said against me
won't amount to anything. If the end brings me out wrong,
ten angels swearing I was right would make no difference.

—ABRAHAM LINCOLN

*Keep away from people who
try to belittle your ambitions.
Small people always do that,
but the really great make you feel that you, too,
can become great.*

—MARK TWAIN

*Let the favor of the Lord our God be upon us
and establish thou the works of our hands upon us.*

—PSALM 90:17 (RSV)

*To me, every hour of the day and night
is an unspeakably perfect miracle.*

—WALT WHITMAN

Commonplace

"A commonplace life," we say, and we sigh,
But why should we sigh as we say?
The commonplace sun in the commonplace sky
Makes up the commonplace day;
The moon and the stars are commonplace things,
And the flower that blooms, and the bird that sings,
But dark were the world, and sad our lot,
If the flowers failed, and the sun shone not;
And God, who studies each separate soul,
Out of commonplace lives makes His beautiful whole.

—SUSAN COOLIDGE

I ought to reflect again and again, and yet again, that
the beings among whom I have to steer are just as inevitable
in the scheme of evolution as I am myself;
have just as much right to be themselves as I am entitled to;
and they all deserve from me as much sympathy as I give to myself.

—ARNOLD BENNETT

If an Arab in the desert were suddenly to discover a spring in his tent,
and so would always be able to have water in abundance, how fortunate
he would consider himself—so too, when a man, who as a
physical being is always turned outside himself, finally turns inward
and discovers that the source is within himself; not to mention
his discovery that the source is his relation to God.

—SØREN KIERKEGAARD

It feels as if everyone who acts compassionately, works to raise
consciousness, to save the planet, to make a difference in some
significant way is linked to everyone else who also does. . . .
Each person who follows his or her own light is a light in the web.

—JEAN SHINODA BOLEN

Old English Prayer

Take time to work—
It is the price of success.
Take time to think—
It is the source of power.
Take time to play—
It is the secret of perpetual youth.
Take time to read—
It is the fountain of wisdom.
Take time to be friendly—
It is the road to happiness.
Take time to dream—
It is hitching your wagon to a star.
Take time to love and be loved—
It is the privilege of the gods.
Take time to look around—
It is too short a day to be selfish.
Take time to laugh—
It is the music of the soul.

—ANONYMOUS

*In every age there is a turning point, a new way of
seeing and asserting the coherence of the world.*
—JACOB BRONOWSKI

*Love all God's creation, both the whole and every grain of sand.
Love every leaf, every ray of light. Love the animals, love the
plants, love each separate thing. If thou love each thing thou will
perceive the mystery of God in all; and when once thou perceive
this, thou wilt thenceforward grow every day to a fuller understanding
of it: until thou come at last to love the whole world with
a love that will then be all-embracing and universal.*
—FYODOR DOSTOEVSKI

*What is your religion? I mean—not what do you know
about religion but the belief that helps you most?*
—GEORGE ELIOT

Artists knock on silence for answering music.
They pursue meaninglessness until they can force it to mean.
—ROLLO MAY

All of us who write work out of a conviction
that we are participating in
some sort of communal activity.
—JOYCE CAROL OATES

All colors are friends of their neighbors
and the lovers of their opposites.
—W. H. AUDEN

Unknowingly, we plough the dust of the stars,
blown around us by the wind,
and drink the universe in a glass of rain.
—IHAB HASSAH

The Artist

The Artist and his Luckless Wife
They lead a horrid haunted life,
Surrounded by the things he's made
That are not wanted by the trade.

The world is very fair to see;
The Artist will not let it be;
He fiddles with the works of God,
And makes them look uncommon odd.

The Artist is an awful man,
He does not do the things he can;
He does the things he cannot do,
And we attend the private view.

The Artist uses honest paint
To represent things as they ain't,
He then asks money for the time
It took to perpetrate the crime.

—SIR WALTER RALEIGH

Artists say: Stop, look, and see what is real.
In our rushing world, no one has time for this.
—LANGDON GILKEY

How to earn money while looking for work is a neat trick.
The bottom line is to face this reality with dignity—
something that provides a lifelong challenge for many of us.
—ALAN THICKE, ACTOR

Write a novel if you must, but think of money
as an unlikely accident.
—PEARL S. BUCK, NOVELIST

I sent Matthew to college to make a gentleman of him,
and he has turned out to be nothing but a damned painter.
—THE FATHER OF ARTIST MATTHEW HARRIS JOUETTE

THE SYMPATHETIC VIBRATION OF LOVE

Love is the most important quality to bring to any task.
Love draws all that we have within us to the action in which
we are involved. It brings trust and acceptance;
it heightens the senses . . . Love does not bring forth
censorship and defensiveness . . . it allows
self-acceptance and total involvement.

—MILDRED PORTNEY CHASE

P lace two identically tuned harps in the same room. Then pluck an A string on one of the harps. Instantly, all the strings tuned to A on both harps will vibrate in sympathetic resonance. When you play a chord on the strings of a guitar or strike the keys of a piano, each note has overtones that vibrate in harmonic resonance and make the music richer. Guitarists who have lived with their instruments for many years find that when sound has "seasoned" the guitar, its resonance, both emotional and musical, is richer. When you walk into the Ryman Auditorium in Nashville, you hear great sound not only because of the physical acoustics of the building, but also because of a resonance that comes from the years of wonderful music played there.

Our lives are like that. We resonate to the things we love, to the people we love. The more we give ourselves permission to love, the more our lives resonate with the overtones of faith, hope, and compassion. The words *community* and *communion* have the same root. We gather together, listen to one another, and then carry that magic back into our everyday lives. We spend quality time alone, choosing to focus on the things that interest us and that we love. We then go out into the community, bringing with us the inner harmonies we have found by becoming at peace with ourselves. It is a cycle of positive feedback. Each choice to be true to the deeper things of the heart helps us become more heartfelt in our approach to life.

> *A great manager has a knack for making ballplayers think*
> *they are better than they think they are. He forces you*
> *to have a good opinion of yourself. He lets you know*
> *he believes in you. And once you learn how good you really are,*
> *you never settle for playing anything less than your very best.*
> —REGGIE JACKSON

The second principle of magic:
. . . things which have once been in contact with each other
continue to act on each other at a distance
after the physical contact has been severed.

—SIR JAMES FRAZER

In quantum physics, scientists have discovered that one quantum object can simultaneously influence its twin object no matter how far apart they may be. Dr. Paul Pearsall, in his book *Wishing Well*, demonstrates how the act of wishing can have a measurable effect on matter. Citing studies from Stanford University and other research institutions, Pearsall shows that focused intention can have an effect on another human being, even at a distance—and that wishing someone well can be beneficial for all concerned. Scientists are discovering what mystics and philosophers have known all along: Consciousness is primary. Not only may material reality be influenced by it, but our consciousness may be the stuff from which material reality comes into being.

What we love, we shall grow to resemble.

—SAINT BERNARD OF CLAIRVAUX

So also in our relationships. Nurturing relationships with time, care, attention, and awareness changes our own lives. Even the difficulties of relationships help us grow. We were created to be part of a community and to share life together. What you are affects your relationships and your relationships affect what you are. It sounds simple and obvious to say that relationships are beneficial, but many times we choose to live in isolation and often treat people as disposable objects instead of sacred beings. We need to tune in and become aware of the people around us, the ways we are interconnected. And we need to acknowledge that love and friendship are mysterious, rich resources that need to be nurtured.

Friendship is not essentially a union of personalities,
it is an attraction and magnetism of souls.
—THOMAS MOORE

In art, and in the higher ranges of science, there is
a feeling of harmony which underlies all endeavor. There is no true
greatness in art or science without that sense of harmony.
—ALBERT EINSTEIN

For there is a music wherever there is a harmony, order,
or proportion; and thus far we may maintain the music
of the spheres; for those well-ordered motions, and regular paces,
though they give no sound unto the ear, yet to the
understanding they strike a note most full of harmony.
—SIR THOMAS BROWNE

For the very universe, it is said, is held together
by a certain harmony of sounds, and the heavens themselves
are made to revolve by the modulation of harmony. . . .
every word we speak, every pulsation of our veins,
is related by musical rhythms to the powers of harmony.
—ISIDORE OF SEVILLE

What we play is life.
—LOUIS ARMSTRONG

The Art of Encouragement

If I were not a physicist, I would probably be a musician.
—ALBERT EINSTEIN

Musical sound lies in the very hearts of the atoms.
—DR. DONALD H. ANDREWS

I like to use the metaphor of music to describe what it is like to develop relationships and to become a person who resonates with the beauty and glory of life. A musician learns techniques and music theory, but the only way to make music is to sit down with your instrument and play. You need to practice for hours on your own, but the greatest fulfillment comes from playing with other instrumentalists, being part of an ensemble or a symphony. From the very beginning, there must be a balance between practicing alone and playing with others. So it should be in our relationships. We develop ourselves and then tune our hearts to be open to others. Our openness and acceptance create a place for friendship to grow. We tune our hearts and train our souls so we can participate in the symphony of life.

On Friday nights you'll often find me at a favorite songwriters' haunt, having a good time with a diverse group of friends. I find that if I am feeling out of tune and tired, I am less able to contribute to the group or appreciate the people around me. If I am out of sorts, they can help me feel better, but I also find that if I've taken time to prepare my heart for giving, I'm more able to appreciate the evening and relate to my friends. If I am at peace with myself, I find I can concentrate on the give-and-take of the group instead of being distracted by my own thoughts. If I am in tune with myself, I play better with others. Making music together means being prepared by knowing your instrument and being in tune.

The essence of all art is having pleasure giving pleasure.
—MIKHAIL BARYSHNIKOV

A symphony and a community both serve the greater whole. It is a pleasure to make music together and to value each individual's part. There are times for solos and times for instruments to play together. There are melody, harmony, counterpoint—and the rests that breathe in the silence between notes. We move together through the measures of passing time.

The next time you are with a group of people, check to see if your heart is in tune. Are you listening to what is being said? Do you hear what is not being said? Do you resonate positively with the group? Are you sensitive when silence is called for? Are you willing to speak up when the need arises? Do you respect yourself and respect others? Is everyone allowed to make a contribution? Are you competing or collaborating? Do these people harmonize with your values? Do you hear the music of life when you are in this community?

Music's not a competitive thing. I don't want to deal
with someone who's in competition with me,
I want to work together and make music.
—EDDIE VAN HALEN

Whether you are playing in the bar, the church,
the strip joint, or the Himalayas, the first duty of music
is to complement and enhance life.
—CARLOS SANTANA

All my thinking about art is haunted by a mystical belief that
in its practice one is tapping sources of truth.
—ROGER HILTON

Love from the center of who you are; don't fake it.
Run for dear life from evil; hold on for dear life to good.
Be good friends who love deeply;
practice playing second fiddle. . . .
Laugh with your happy friends when they're happy;
share tears when they're down. Get along with each other;
don't be stuck-up. Make friends with nobodies;
don't be the great somebody.
Don't hit back; discover beauty in everyone.
—ROMANS 12: 9–10,15–17 (THE MESSAGE)

How you play a note is just as important
as what that note is.
—HENRY KAISER

Encouraging
Ourselves

It is never too late to be what you might have been.

—GEORGE ELIOT

SOUP FOR THE SOUL, TEA FOR THE SPIRIT

Teach us delight in simple things.

—RUDYARD KIPLING

I t's a cold, wet day, with rain turning to sleet, and snow is expected by nightfall. Normally I wouldn't mind the weather because I work out of my home. I can batten down the hatches and ride out the storm, never having to stick my nose out the door except for a chosen appointment or activity. But today I am feeling frustrated, restless with cabin fever. I've stayed home and worked hard over the last several days. Now I want to spend time with friends at our weekly gathering, when we sit in a café and eat, talk, laugh, and listen to music. It's my favorite songwriters' night in Nashville, and I was planning on going as my reward for a long, intense workweek.

But, unfortunately, a cold front is moving in and the rain is turning to a wintry mix of sleet and snow. Driving to the other side of town could be treacherous, and Nashville drivers aren't used to snow and ice. If it gets too snowy, the café will close early. Snow days are infrequent in the South, so in wintry conditions, wise drivers stay off the roads when at all possible.

I look out the window and see wet gray. I hear the *slop-slosh* of tires as cars pass my front door, windshield wipers going full tilt and headlights glowing in the gathering dusk. I have a choice to make. What will I do about this unexpected kink in my festive plans? Will I slump passively in front of the TV, grumbling because my big social night is a bust? Or will I find other ways to re-energize my weary soul? After an intense week of writing, I need a break.

It's time to do a little self-nurturing, some physical encouragement after all that concentrated mental work. Time to make a pot of onion soup, complete with crusty bread and bubbling-hot cheese on top.

I stop, take a breath, and let go of my anxious agenda. I realize that I have been squeezing myself into production mode instead of enjoying the process of creating a book. Deadlines, demands on my time, lack of energy, and my own limitations have caused my wider vision of the work to narrow to a too-tight focus on production instead of process. Now, as I pull focus and step back from my need to produce so many pages in an allotted time, I realize that I have been subtly losing the soul of what I dreamed of communicating to my readers.

As I chop and sauté onions and add seasonings and broth, creating a delicious dish-for-one that will both nourish and nurture, I remember that my creative work is itself a soulful broth. I am the writer/chef, serving up a tasty dish for my readers—a morsel of quote here, a sip of idea there, a seasoning of attitude adjustment added to the mix. A new serenity permeates my day and renewed wisdom flows out onto my page. In the act of trying to distill encouragement on the page, I had forgotten to encourage and comfort myself. Now a steaming pot of soup reminds me that I must fill my own well in order to quench the thirst of others. I need to let go of my agendas and schedules, to give God room to surprise me and my soul room to expand.

Alexandra Stoddard, in her book *Tea Celebrations*, reminds me that "when we pay attention to little things a universal energy flows through our present, magnifying the meaning of events." A Zen tea-master, she says, is a master of the art of living. The tea-master notices the subtle beauty of the commonplace, raising this awareness to the level of art. This is a way to nurture the soul, allowing us to value the moment, here and now—this specific choice, this curved bowl of soup, this pencil running across the page, this time of being enclosed in a cocoon of winter weather.

I have wanted to grow as a writer, and as a person. In sharing this quiet decision to give my soul some breathing space, I now see that if I am to be a better writer, I must write about what is real for me. If I am to encourage others, I must first fill my inner well and encourage myself. In a world that prefers great accomplishments and ignores small moments, I must remember that the small moments are important, the little choices count. If there are to be any great accomplishments, they begin with what we choose to do in the moment-by-moment decisions of our lives.

Wayne Muller, author of *Sabbath*, insists that we are all too frazzled in this fast-paced, quick-results society. We do not make wise decisions because we make them with a fight-or-flight sense of urgency. We are too tired and stressed to pay attention, to sense the deeper solution to a problem. Social workers are often so overwhelmed by the urgent needs of their clients and by their own work agendas that they cannot be still long enough to discover the solution inherent in a problem. In fact, the need to solve the problem as quickly as possible often produces a "solution" that only creates another problem.

Muller recommends that we return to the ancient practice of Sabbath, taking time off for refreshment, delight, and honoring the rhythms of our lives. Whether we take one day out of seven for Sabbath rest or just a few hours or moments in our day, we can find wisdom and renewal in a time of quietness and peace. It gives us an opportunity to hold still long enough to let things settle, to find clarity in our situation, and to allow a deeper, more timeless wisdom to speak to our hearts.

A bowl of homemade soup, a cup of tea, a soul-break in my day—these are ways to allow God to encourage me and fill my heart again. When I allow time for this in my life, I find that I return to my tasks and relationships more serene and more aware of nuances I would have missed in my hurried, weary rush to cross another task off my to-do list.

I encourage you to take time to savor your life. Take a break. Rest your tired body. Relax your tired soul. Let go of your busy agenda and acknowledge that God is capable of running the universe without your help. Rest in His goodness, and allow the peace to permeate your soul. Make a pot of tea; prepare a bowl of soup; knead a loaf of bread; pray. Go for a walk in the woods, listen to music, make love, take a bath, read a book just for the fun of it, gaze at the full moon, spend time with a friend, or take a nap. See what a quiet moment can offer to your heart. Like a Zen tea-master, choose to practice the art of living.

> *To go fishing is the chance to wash one's soul with pure air,*
> *with the rush of the brook, or with the shimmer of the sun*
> *on blue water. It brings meekness and inspiration*
> *from the decency of nature, charity toward tackle-makers,*
> *patience toward fish, a mockery of profits and egos,*
> *a quieting of hate, a rejoicing that you do not have to decide*
> *a darned thing until next week. And it is discipline*
> *in the equality of men—for all men are equal before fish.*
>
> —HERBERT HOOVER

Whatever peace I know rests in the natural world,
in feeling myself a part of it, even in a small way.
—MAY SARTON

Take time to come home to yourself every day.
—ROBIN CASARJEAN

Meditation is nothing but coming back home,
just to have a little rest inside.
—OSHO

All the Arabs reverence a man's sleeping;
he is as it were in trance with God,
and a truce of his waking solicitude:
in their households they piously withdraw,
nor will any lightly molest him,
until he waken of himself.
—CHARLES M. DOUGHTY

Health is the first muse, and sleep is the condition to produce it.
—RALPH WALDO EMERSON

Have courage for the great sorrows of life
and patience for the small ones;
and when you have laboriously
accomplished your daily task,
go to sleep in peace. God is awake.
—VICTOR HUGO

Unless the Lord builds the house,
those who build it labor in vain.
Unless the Lord watches over the city,
the watchman stays awake in vain.
It is in vain that you rise up early
and go late to rest,
eating the bread of anxious toil:
for he gives to his beloved in sleep.
—PSALM 127:1–2 (RSV)

A man should hear a little music, read a little poetry,
and see a fine picture every day of his life,
in order that worldly cares may not obliterate
the sense of the beautiful which God
has implanted in the human soul.

—GOETHE

It is fun to get together and have something good to eat
at least once a day. That's what human life is all about—
enjoying things.

—JULIA CHILD

No matter what looms ahead, if you can eat today,
enjoy the sunlight today, mix good cheer with friends today,
enjoy it and bless God for it.

—HENRY WARD BEECHER

When shall we live if not now?

—M. F. K. FISHER

To finish the moment,
to find the journey's end in every step of the road,
to live the greatest number of good hours, is wisdom.
—RALPH WALDO EMERSON

Life is not lost by dying; life is lost minute by minute,
day by day, in all the thousand small uncaring ways.
—STEPHEN VINCENT BENÉT

Wake at dawn with a winged heart and
give thanks for another day of loving.
—KAHLIL GIBRAN

No more words. In the name of this place we drink
in with our breathing, stay quiet like a flower.
So the nightbirds will start singing.
—RUMI

To pray is to take notice of the wonder,
to regain a sense of the mystery that animates all beings,
the divine margin in all our attainments.
—ABRAHAM JOSHUA HESCHEL

It is in deep solitude and silence that I find the gentleness
with which I can truly love my brother and my sister.
—THOMAS MERTON

I have in my heart a small shy plant called reverence;
I cultivate that on Sunday morning.
—OLIVER WENDELL HOLMES

Reverence is the very first element of religion;
it cannot but be felt by every one who has right views
of the divine greatness and holiness, and of his own
character in the sight of God.
—CHARLES SIMMONS

The dullest observer must be sensible of the order
and serenity prevalent in those households where
the occasional exercise of a beautiful form of worship
in the morning gives, as it were, the keynote to every temper
for the day, and attunes every spirit to harmony.
—WASHINGTON IRVING

Through the week we go down into the valleys of care
and shadow. Our Sabbaths should be hills of light and joy in God's
presence; and so as time rolls by we shall go on from
mountain top to mountain top, till at last we catch the glory of
the gate, and enter in to go no more out forever.
—HENRY WARD BEECHER

The Sabbath is God's present to the working man, and one of its
chief objects is to prolong his life, and preserve efficient his working tone.
The savings bank of human existence is the weekly Sabbath.
—WILLIAM G. BLAIKIE

We doctors, in the treatment of nervous diseases,
are now constantly compelled to prescribe periods of rest.
Some periods are, I think, only Sundays in arrears.

—SIR JAMES CRICHTON–BROWNE

Some keep Sabbath by going to church;
I keep it staying at home,
With a bobolink for a chorister,
And an orchard for a dome.

—EMILY DICKINSON

The green oasis,
the little grassy meadow in the wilderness;
where, after the weekday's journey,
the pilgrim halts for refreshment and repose.

—CHARLES READE

Only in the oasis of silence can we drink deeply
from our inner cup of wisdom.

—SUE PATTON THOELE

Sitting quietly, doing nothing.
Spring comes, and the grass grows by itself.

—ZEN PROVERB

The seed of mystery lies in muddy water.
How can I perceive this mystery?
Water becomes clear through stillness.
How can I become still?
By flowing with the stream.

—LAO-TZU

Be still, and know that I am God.

—PSALM 46:10 (KJV)

A few favorite resources that nurture my soul:

Tea Celebrations: The Way to Serenity
Alexandra Stoddard

Gift from the Sea
Anne Morrow Lindbergh

Pilgrim at Tinker Creek
Annie Dillard

If You Want to Write
Brenda Ueland

A Natural History of the Senses
Diane Ackerman

Cloister Walk
Kathleen Norris

Spiritual Literacy: Reading the Sacred in Everyday Life
Frederic and Mary Ann Brussat

Sabbath
Wayne Muller

The Supper of the Lamb
Robert Farrar Capon

Walking on Water
Madeleine L'Engle

Jenny Walton's Packing for a Woman's Journey
Nancy Lindemeyer

Traveling Mercies
Anne Lamott

In Search of Stones
M. Scott Peck

Other favorite authors of mine include:

Fredrich Buechner

Robert Benson

Gunilla Norris

M. F. K. Fisher

Thomas Merton

Edith Schaefer

G. K. Chesterton

Henri Nouwen

Sam Keen

Eugene Peterson

Wendell Berry

Paul Tournier

John O'Donohue

C. S. Lewis

Other great sources of renewal:

Poetry collections

Quotation books

Children's books

Travel magazines and books

Memoirs

Nature books

Cozy novels

Gardening and cookbooks

Movies

A great Web site for researching good books, movies, and videos for nurturing the spirit is www.spiritualrx.com.

PERMISSION GRANTED

Think of yourself as an incandescent power, illuminated and perhaps forever talked to by God and His messengers.

—BRENDA UELAND

You have permission to be who you are. You have permission to love what you love. You have permission to be with the people you wish to be with and to do the things you want to do. You have permission to ask questions, to experience all the pains and pleasures of your life.

You have permission to listen to your body's needs and to meet those needs. You have permission to explore your inner heart. You do not have to separate yourself into airtight compartments labeled *body*, *mind*, *soul*, *spirit*. You have permission to be a whole person, not a fragmented collection of miscellaneous parts.

You have permission to wait for divine guidance. Divine Source gives you permission to be who you are right now—and will help you become all that you were born to be. God is an artist and you are a work of art, unique and beautiful. You are a work of art in progress, a divine poem being written on the pages of time.

You don't have to twist yourself into a pretzel to become someone you are not. You don't have to squeeze yourself into a tight little box to fit someone else's expectations. The universe has given you permission to be yourself.

Breathe a sigh of relief. Let go of what you have been holding onto so tightly. Open your hands and release your spirit. Let the Divine Presence enter the temple of your heart. Allow healing to begin. Allow growth and change to happen. It will be all right. Let life flow through the center of your being. Bask in the sunlight of God's love. You are beloved and you are becoming. God is removing all obstacles, all stumbling blocks, all sin, disappointment, and failure. You have spent too much time beating yourself up for the wrong reasons. No one needs to tell you about your sins, your shortcomings, and all the times you failed to make the right decision and follow through on it. You know these things in your heart of hearts. Your very cells carry the memory and the pain.

But God does not leave you in your misery. His divine intent is life—God is the fullness of life itself, and you share in that fullness. The source that drives the green shoot of spring's new life wants also to fill you with that renewing life. Healing, forgiveness, and refreshment are there for you. Open your heart and open your hands—you will receive.

You have permission to receive this loving flow of energy and healing.

You do not have to earn it, or buy it, or steal it from someone else. The ever-flowing fountain of life streams from the center of your heart, from the hidden springs of your being. You just need to rest, rest, rest. Be still in the silence of God's love and acceptance.

You already possess everything necessary to become great.
—CROW PROVERB

Arise, shine, for your light has come, and the glory of the Lord rises upon you.
—ISAIAH 60:1 (NIV)

The little girl had tossed all night in her bed, feverish and in great pain. No cool cloths could soothe the restless body. No word of hope could reach her in her delirium. Then, as the hot, dusty afternoon turned to dusk, she grew quiet. Her flushed cheeks turned pale, her breath became shallow and labored. Friends and family began to weep, realizing that only a slender thread tied the sick girl to life.

She became silent and still—no breath, no struggle—just the waxen face of death, like a candle with no flame. Then He entered the room. An intake of breath, a small sigh, a sudden flush as blood began to color her cheeks. Her waxen lips grew rosy as her heart began to pump renewed life through her arteries. He dismissed the wailing relatives and mourners and walked over to the bed. He said, "Little girl, get up."

The minute He came through the doorway, it was as if Life itself had entered that room of death. Life had walked into the room, and when He spoke, her spirit responded to the command. As a flower turns toward the sun, the little girl opened her eyes and looked into His. She reached up and He took her hand. It was as if a flow of energy was pouring through Him into her body. Heart spoke to heart in that moment. The little girl smiled, sighed again, and held His hand tightly. For the rest of her life, she would remember that face smiling down at her, bringing her to life, giving her the power to grow in love and to flower into her full potential as wife, mother, grandmother—and as a creative woman who knew she had a work to do in her life, for she had received divine permission from Life Himself.

When a great moment knocks on the door of your life, very often it's no louder than the beating of your heart, and it's very easy to miss it.

—BORIS PASTERNAK

For how can a man know God without yielding himself
fully to the processes of God?

—DAVID GRAYSON

When Jesus was still speaking, someone came from the house of Jairus, the synagogue ruler. "Your daughter is dead," he said. "Don't bother the teacher any more."

Hearing this, Jesus said to Jairus, "Don't be afraid. Just believe, and she will be healed."

When he arrived at the house of Jairus, he did not let anyone go in with him except Peter, John, and James, and the child's father and mother. Meanwhile, all the people were wailing and mourning for her. "Stop wailing," Jesus said. "She is not dead but asleep."

They laughed at him, knowing that she was dead. But he took her by the hand and said, "My child, get up!" Her spirit returned, and at once she stood up. Then Jesus told them to give her something to eat. Her parents were astonished, but he ordered them not to tell anyone what had happened.

—LUKE 8:49–56 (NIV)

RECIPES FOR RECOLLECTION

*Learn to get in touch with the silence within yourself
and know that everything in this life has a purpose.*
—ELISABETH KÜBLER-ROSS

P rayer and meditation are crucial to practicing the art of encouragement. You need to take time to fill your own well, listen to your own
heart, and hear the still, small voice of God before you can reach out to others.
Quiet time in solitude clears the mind. And small breaks in the day help you
focus on work that must be done. Here are a few suggestions for simple ways
to remember your spirit and re-collect your thoughts.

*Prayer is not an old woman's idle amusement.
Properly understood and applied,
it is the most potent instrument of action.*
—MAHATMA GANDHI

LISTEN TO YOUR HEART.

Stressed out? Take a deep breath. Now put your right hand on your heart and cover it with your left hand. Close your eyes. Feel your heart beating, cradled beneath your two hands. Sit quietly for a few minutes with your eyes closed, breathing gently in and out. Think about those you love or about something dear to your heart. If you feel so led, pray about what is troubling you, a special concern, or something you are thankful for today. Listen to what your heart is telling you. Rest quietly before you open your eyes.

LOOK AT A ROSE.

Put one rose in a vase and place it in front of you. If you can be bathed in sunlight while doing this exercise, so much the better. Take time to really look at the rose, to see its intricate beauty. Look at the way the petals fold in on one another in a complex pattern of spiraling beauty. Gaze into the heart of the rose. Take time to really see it and savor the sight. See the shimmering life of the petals. Image the cells growing, expanding, multiplying. Feel the lifeforce of the blossom. Imagine the garden where its life began, the way its death can feed other roses through the gift of compost. Imagine the hands that worked to grow the rose and bring it to you. Think about your life as a rose unfolding. Experience the rose with all your senses.

You can contemplate other things as well: flowers, plants, seashells, a candle flame, a sleeping kitten, fish swimming in an aquarium.

GAZE AT A FACE.

Apply the preceding exercise to the face of someone you know. Imagine how a stranger would see her or him. How would you feel if this were the last time you were ever to see this person? Absorb the beauty and strength of your friend. Listen to what this person is saying to you. Listen with your heart, with focused intention. Look and listen as a lover. Remember their struggles, identify with their weaknesses, and appreciate their gifts.

Look at the faces of strangers. See their infinite variety. Look at noses and eyes and body types and styles. What kind of day are they having? What stories can you make up about where they have come from or where they are going? Imagine what it would be like to know these strangers as intimate friends. See them through the eyes of a loving and compassionate God. Value them for their uniqueness—and for their humanity, as they share common struggles and triumphs.

BE LIKE SCARLETT O'HARA: WORRY ABOUT IT TOMORROW.

Scarlett would say, "I'll think about that tomorrow." When you have a multitude of concerns, choose just one to work with today. Set aside all the others and concentrate with your whole being on the one task you have chosen. Do not allow other concerns to steal focus. This can be very restful and empowering. It is soothing and healing to focus on one thing at a time, giving your full attention to whatever you are doing. It is a way to live in the here and now, and to make a conscious choice about where you want to focus your attention.

Mothers of babies, toddlers, and preschoolers, who have to juggle a multitude of tasks at once, may have great difficulty doing this exercise. In this busy season of your life, this tip may not be possible to apply, other than in brief moments, usually geared to the attention span of a two-year-old. Understand that certain seasons of life are more full of distractions, and apply this recipe for recollection accordingly.

CREATE A MOMENT AND SHARE IT.

Set the table. Make a centerpiece of flowers. Light candles. Prepare a meal and arrange it—or fast food, defrosted frozen entrée, or deli takeout—attractively on pretty plates. Let your loved ones know that dining with them is a special occasion.

Other ideas for shared moments:
- Take the family to the beach to watch a sunset together or to stargaze on a clear, warm night.
- Get together with a friend for a cup of tea.
- Take a walk with friends or family in the neighborhood or park and enjoy the season.
- Go to a worship service together.
- Celebrate life with simple gifts.
- Buy yourself a single rose. Buy one to give to a friend.
- Send a card or note for no particular reason—just "because."
- Bake someone a batch of their favorite cookies.
- Treat someone to a cup of coffee and a doughnut (or carrot juice and an oatmeal bar, for the health-conscious).
- Give someone a book that is meaningful to you.
- Make a tape of your favorite music for a friend to enjoy.
- Give the gift of your time and attention.

METABOLIZING CRITICISM

It requires great daring to dare to be oneself.

—EUGENE DELACROIX

Nashville is a town of music critics. Some of the best songwriters and musicians in the world live here—music is big business. Criticism and comparison can become a way of life here, because we are inundated with opportunities to hear top players, the *crème de la crème* of the field. That's true for any place where creative specialists gather. New York and L.A. have their own fishbowls where everyone is looking for the latest, hottest thing and discarding yesterday's hits like so much old newspaper for recycling. Since criticism is a fact of life, you have to learn how to deal with it.

I was at a songwriters' night recently; five people were featured for the evening. There were over fifty people in that packed room. And ninety percent of the audience were gifted songwriters and musicians, all of whom have spent a lifetime working on their musical chops and honing their writing craft. This particular venue offers one of the most supportive audiences in the world, because everyone knows what it takes to get this far and to be performing for this particular group of peers. But it is also the most critical audience in the world. They appreciate the craft, learn from the songs presented, and judge songs by the standards of both craft and heart, and by how the performer's music stacks up against their own work.

Many times, the person performing may be singing his or her song to a hero in the audience—someone who has written a classic or has had big hits or is influential in the music industry. It can be intimidating to play for such an audience, even one that offers the warm reception that this one does. It is even tougher to play for a critical audience of publishers and/or record label executives. Yes, if Nashville is your hometown, you had better be prepared to handle criticism when you play.

A friend just sent me her newly minted CD. It's gorgeous—as gorgeous as she is. Western swing, up-tempo, and fun, though Music Row considers it an old-fashioned style right now. (They don't feel that way down in the Texas dance halls, I hear.) Her music has a timeless feel; it's well crafted, with a quality that matches the best of what Music Row can produce. She had some of the finest studio musicians in the world play on her album and it shows.

She's good, too. As good as the backup musicians are, they never overshadow her voice, which sparkles and shimmers. She's a great looking, hard-working lady who has been paying her dues for years. To look at the whole package, you'd bet she's got a surefire formula for success.

But the music business is not that simple or logical. In fact, life is not that simple or logical. Success can be defined in many ways. If you are thinking "hit radio, big record label, arena-tour" success, my friend isn't currently at that level. Her project was self-financed, and she's the artist, booking agent, tour manager, publicist, and financial backer—no other staff except an encouraging husband, who is also a songwriter/musician.

Success at a big record label can come with a high price tag, however. It takes a special combination of persistence, talent, timing, and lucky breaks to achieve international success. And sometimes achieving success means selling your soul—or at least letting the record label control your career and your life. At this time in her life, success for my talented friend means completing a project that expresses her musical soul and that she can own and control herself.

She has labored long and hard to bring this dream to fruition. Now comes the time for dealing with criticism and myriad opinions. Some people will love it. Some people may hate it. Some people will prefer another style.

Many people may be indifferent. But, somewhere out there, she'll find an appreciative audience.

Because her project is outstanding and professionally competitive, she has a chance of catching the attention of influential ears. But, because she doesn't have money to hire a publicist or a radio promotion expert, she will have a more difficult time reaching those influential listeners.

With persistence and hard work, my friend can build success through sales and touring, creating a self-sustaining career. It's being done all the time by independent artists. Her success may not mean millions of dollars or superstardom, but she'll probably be able to finance her next CD project, build a regional audience, and sing to appreciative crowds. She might even provoke interest from a major record label. This current completed project is only one step in a long line of choices and opportunities.

So what does my friend do about rejection, which is inevitable in this business? What do any of us do, for that matter, about the rejection and negative criticism that come whenever we step out and take a risk?

The first thing to remember is that you must yourself be satisfied with your work, knowing you've done the best you could do with what you had to work with at the time. Know that, if you're worth your salt, you'll always wish you could do more, improve, become more proficient at your craft or skill.

Those who do good work of any kind always seem to be seeking that next mountain to climb, that next challenge that takes them to another creative level. But it is crucial to find satisfaction in your work at this time and at this stage of your development. Be gentle and generous with yourself. Give credit where credit is due. Do not let that inner voice of censorship overwhelm you with self-defeating criticism.

Be thankful that you have completed a task and then move on. Recognize that this is one step in a long process. You do not stand or fall by one project, one performance, one public appearance. This is not "make or break"—this is a signpost, a landmark on a long journey. If you look at successful people, you'll see that the majority work patiently at what they do over the long term. You'll find that everyone has their ups and downs, but it's the ones who keep going that get somewhere. Trust the process.

Love what you do. Give yourself permission to do something for the sheer love of it. When love is your motivation, others' opinions matter less. The fire is generated from inside, from the center of your heart.

Love is the compass that guides you across the desert stretches and through the howling wilderness. If you love what you do, you will be able to move beyond your own fears and the negative opinions of others. There is no substitute for passionate and heartfelt belief.

Listen to your intuition. You know when criticism is valid and helpful. You also know instinctively when criticism is a personal attack. If the criticism helps you do what you do better, gives you greater insight into your work, or resonates with your deepest feelings, pay attention. If the criticism is careless or vindictive, it might reflect the critic's own inner struggles. There is no one crueler than a blocked artist who uses criticism as a weapon to cut other artists down to size. Your intuition will tell you if you're in the presence of one of these troubled souls.

Realize also that critics are fallible human beings and that there is no all-encompassing, perfect system that takes all factors into account. When a critic for *Music Row* magazine skewers a CD in a review, he's comparing it to all the CDs that have crossed his desk, including the latest by the hottest artist at the biggest label in town. If my friend decides to have her CD reviewed by the magazine, she knows that the music critic will be listening according to certain criteria of excellence, and that he'll be listening to the end product, not the story of the struggle to create it. When someone criticizes you, remember what standards he or she may be using. Your mother will judge you by one standard, your friends and peers by others, and professional critics by yet another.

Remember that many great and lasting talents have been skewered by the critics. This year's critic's darling may be next year's whipping boy. Some seasons, your work is hot; some seasons, your work is ignored or trashed. You never know. What matters is that you stay true to yourself, encourage yourself, believe in your best dreams, and follow your highest intentions. Do not judge the work—just keep doing it.

And while a professional critic may be an expert in the field, he or she also has personal preferences, good and bad days, ups and downs. If your precious project crosses the critic's desk on the day he's had an argument with his wife, he'll listen to it differently than he will on a day when he's just received a raise.

All voices of criticism, at all times, are human and subjective. Because the arts are so subjective, artists of all kinds have to learn to take criticism with a saltshaker full of salt—and then move on. Many stop reading the critiques after a while so they can avoid distraction and put their energy into concentrating on their work.

Even though you may not have a music publisher cutting off your precious-baby song in midmeasure and announcing that it's not what he's looking for right now, you will face criticism from others, at work and in your personal life. Know that each person who criticizes is human and fallible. Listen respectfully and separate the gold from the dross. Be glad for solid and helpful criticism, and be aware of hidden agendas behind the criticism. Never, ever let criticism stop you from following your heart or going for the highest good in a situation.

One last note on criticism, careers, and reaching your goals: In the long run, it is about the long run. It is about process, not product. Do you love what you do? Then do it. Do you want to learn more and improve? Then invest in yourself and take your dreams seriously. Enjoy the process. Enjoy doing the creative work or collaborating with others or making a difference in some small way. Enjoy raising your voice in the chorus of creation, playing your instrument in the symphony of life. God sees. God knows. Open your heart to Him and listen as He applauds.

As for my friend with the bright, shiny new CD? I venture to predict that by the time this book reaches your hands, she will have garnered reviews both positive and negative. She will have booked some concerts in her hometown and created a Web site to make her music available on the Internet. Some of her connections will turn up new opportunities. Some of the people she connects with will help her get somewhere, some will lead to detours, some to dead ends. Unexpected opportunities may come from out of the blue. And some new door of opportunity may open up even as another door closes.

Whether a major label comes calling or she builds a feisty independent career, she'll follow her heart and find her way in the world. Whatever happens, I know this beautiful and talented woman will keep on singing, keep on finding ways to make creative music, and have a ball doing it.

*That best picture has not yet been painted; the greatest poem is
still unsung; the mightiest novel remains to be written;
the divinest music has not been conceived even by Bach.
In science, probably ninety-nine percent of the knowable
has not yet been discovered.*
—LINCOLN STEFFENS

*The pessimist sees difficulty in every opportunity;
the optimist, the opportunity in every difficulty.*
—L. P. JACKS

IDEAS FOR METABOLIZING CRITICISM

Here are a few suggestions for working criticism through your system. It is always important to nurture yourself, cradle your heart, and give things time to settle. I have found these ideas to be great for coping with both negative and positive criticism. They ground you and keep you from losing perspective.

❖ Take long walks.

❖ Write in your journal and be honest about how you feel. Let your journal be your safe place where you can vent and work through your feelings.

❖ Get plenty of rest. During stressful times, naps are essential.

❖ Drink lots of water, eat sensibly, and take care of your body.

❖ Spend time with friends who believe in you.

❖ Start your next creative project. This is very empowering and takes pressure off the current project.

❖ Immerse yourself in satisfying work or happy play.

❖ Laugh.

❖ Go see a movie or escape into a good book.

❖ Acknowledge that the criticism hurt. Allow yourself a brief time in which to lick your wounds, then move on. Do not dwell on negative thoughts or allow the pain to escalate into self-pity.

❖ Be aware of the critic's hidden agendas. Is this constructive criticism or is it meant to cut you down to size?

❖ Listen to your intuition. Trust your deepest instincts. Your heart knows more than your brain does—listen to it.

- ❖ Take a break and get away. You'll come back refreshed, with a better perspective.
- ❖ Pet a cat or dog. Let an animal's unconditional love soothe your lacerated feelings.
- ❖ Get out into nature—the more magnificent, the better. There is nothing like mountains or the ocean or a vast, open sky to put things into perspective.
- ❖ Look for others who have survived rejection and created their own success. These could be people you know and admire, or heroes you read about in books and magazines. Inspirational stories can keep you from giving up.
- ❖ Balance solitude and sociability. Take some quiet time to be alone, to think about your life. Then find a good friend or a good party, to remind you that you are not alone.
- ❖ Feed your soul. Listen to great music, read great books, go to an art gallery or a museum, walk in a formal garden.
- ❖ See yourself as one drop in the infinite stream of human endeavor. Look at the varieties of expression and remember that there is something for every taste.
- ❖ Read a classic children's book and escape the cold, cruel adult world for an hour or two.

❖ Watch a child learn to walk.

❖ Write a list of your hundred favorite things: pink roses, iced tea in tall frosty glasses, Renoir paintings, the sound of ocean waves, sappy old movies, a certain person's smile, etc.

❖ Make a list of personal accomplishments, large and small: learning to change the car's oil, winning an art award in junior high, moving to a new town, taking music lessons, auditioning for a play, etc.

Accept that some days you're the pigeon, and some days you're the statue.
—ROGER C. ANDERSON

❖ Read bad poetry, watch an awful B movie, and be reminded that really, really bad art has contributed a great deal of pleasure to our lives. I take a perverse pleasure in the awfulness of some things—sometimes they are so bad they're wonderful. How poor the world would be without Roger Corman movies and Victorian parlor poetry!

❖ I love bad movies: *Attack of the Killer Tomatoes*, *Bambi versus Godzilla*, Monty Python sketches, *Will Success Spoil Rock Hunter?* (with Tony Randall and Jayne Mansfield), and that wonderful classic, *Young Frankenstein:*

"What was the name of the brain I put in the monster?"

"Uh, Abby something."

"Abby something?"

"Uh, Abby Normal."

Some favorite movie selections for a good laugh:

* *Teenagers from Outer Space*: "Oh, Derek," cries the very white-bread Betty as the young alien (who looks a lot like Harry Connick Jr.) dies to stop his companions from importing "gargons" (fifties-style special effects lobsters) to graze on the planet and destroy mankind.

* *Queen of Outer Space*: In this turkey, Earth spacemen land on Venus and find sexy Venusian soldier-women in high heels and short skirts (they look like fifties carhops carrying rifles). The queen of Venus, their leader, is none other than Zsa Zsa Gabor, in a classic performance. "Dahlink, you earthmen must not disturb our peaceful female society."

* *Attack of the Eye Creatures*: These aliens are covered with eyes and look pretty dorky as they descend on a carload of fifties teenagers making out in their huge, gas-guzzling cars. I adore bad special effects.

* Annette Funicello and Frankie Avalon or Annette and Tommy Kirk in any of those old, bad, beach-party movies. Or sixties ski-party movies. Youth

having canned fun, complete with corny music and non-existent plots. You gotta love Annette's big hair. (I adored her as a Mouseketeer and wanted to be like her when I grew up.)

❖ Other movie titles that sound so bad they're good: *The Crawling Eye*, *The Robot vs. the Aztec Mummy*, *Godzilla vs. the Sea Monster*, *Pod People*, *Kitten with a Whip* (starring Ann-Margret as the kitten), *The Amazing Colossal Man*, *It Conquered the World* (featuring Beverly Garland), *Earth vs. the Spider*, *Teenage Cave Man* (starring Robert Vaughn), *Viking Women and the Sea Serpent*, *Santa Claus Conquers the Martians*, *Attack of the Giant Leeches*, *Hercules Unchained*, *Fire Maidens of Outer Space*, *Monster a Go-Go*, *Bride of the Monster* (a tender romance), *The Brain That Wouldn't Die*, and *The Amazing Transparent Man*.

I never forget a face. But in your case, I'll make an exception.
—GROUCHO MARX

❖ Look for Internet sites that unabashedly celebrate the not-so-very-good in life. The constantly changing Weird Wide Web has something for everyone. A few of the sites that make me laugh: www.sweetpotatoqueens. com, www.fishydance.com, www.dullmen.com, and who could ever forget the exciting revelations of the www.cowcam, when cams were hot and the Internet was young? Other sites that will lead you to an infinite number of silly and humorous Web sites are www.amused.com and www.uselesssites.com.

Everything is funny as long as it is happening to someone else.
—WILL ROGERS

Total absence of humor renders life impossible.
—COLETTE

❖ *The Incomplete Book of Failures*, by Stephen Pile, is "The Official Handbook of the Not Terribly Good Club of Great Britain." I found this classic collection of colossal failures in my local library (it's out of print, but Amazon.com lists it). The author says, "Success is overrated. Everyone craves it despite daily proof that man's real genius lies in quite the opposite direction. Incompetence is what we are good at: it is the quality that marks us off from animals and we should learn to revere it."

Here are some other resources for cultivating the truly awful: *Very Bad Poetry*, edited by Kathryn Petras and Ross Petras. Vintage Books, 1997.

The Art of Encouragement

Parlour Poetry: A Casquet of Gems, selected and introduced by Michael Turner. Viking Press, 1969.

The Mystery Science Theater 3000 Amazing Colossal Episode Guide, by Best Brains, Inc. Bantam Books, 1996.

The Portable Curmudgeon and *The Portable Curmudgeon Redux*, compiled and edited by Jon Winokur. Dutton Publishing.

Alexander and the Terrible, Horrible, No Good, Very Bad Day, by Judith Viorst, is written for kids, but adults can use this antidote to miserable days, too. Atheneum Publishing, 1972.

Rejection, by John White. Addison-Wesley Publishing, 1982.

Check the humor section at your local library or bookstore for more treasures.

What is the voice of song, when the world lacks the ear of taste?
—NATHANIEL HAWTHORNE

We don't like their sound. Groups with guitars are on the way out.
—DECCA RECORDING COMPANY, REJECTING THE BEATLES

Wagner's music is better than it sounds.
—MARK TWAIN

114

I played over the music of that scoundrel Brahms. What a giftless bastard.
—PETER ILICH TCHAIKOVSKY

If Beethoven's Seventh Symphony is not by some means abridged,
it will soon fall into disuse.
—PHILIP HALE

I like Beethoven, especially the poems.
—RINGO STARR

Sousa was no Beethoven. Nonetheless, he was Sousa.
—DEEMS TAYLOR

Fred Astaire was described by one studio that rejected him as
a balding, skinny actor who can dance a little.

Thomas Edison's first teacher called him "addled," and others
said he would never make a success of anything.

Einstein's parents were afraid he was retarded.
A teacher told him he would never amount to anything.

Puccini, the great composer, had a music teacher who said
that he had no talent and gave up on him.

The University of Vienna rejected Gregor Mendel,
the founder of genetics. One of his professors wrote,
"Mendel lacks the requisite clarity of thought to be a scientist."

*Flight by machines heavier than air is unpractical and
insignificant, if not utterly impossible.*
—SIMONE NEWCOMB, ASTRONOMER
(EIGHTEEN MONTHS BEFORE THE WRIGHT BROTHERS FLEW)

*Young man, you can be grateful that my invention is not for sale,
for it would undoubtedly ruin you. It can be exploited for a certain time as a
scientific curiosity, but apart from that it has no commercial value whatsoever.*
—AUGUSTE LUMIÈRE (COMMENTING ON MOVING PICTURES IN 1895)

It will never be possible to synchronize the voice with the pictures.
. . . There will never be speaking pictures.
—D. W. GRIFFITH (1924)

Who the hell wants to hear actors talk?
—H. M. WARNER

Americans require a restful quiet in the moving picture theater,
and for them talking . . . on the screen destroys the illusion.
—THOMAS EDISON

The movie actor, like the sacred king of primitive tribes, is a god in captivity.
—ALEXANDER CHASE

Actors are cattle.
—ALFRED HITCHCOCK

The real actor—like any real artist—has a direct line to the collective heart.
—BETTE DAVIS

Players, Sir! I look at them as no better than creatures set upon tables and joint stools to make faces and produce laughter, like dancing dogs.

—SAMUEL JOHNSON

The better the actor the more stupid he is.

—TRUMAN CAPOTE

With me it was 5 percent talent and 95 percent publicity.

—MARION DAVIES

She has two expressions: joy and indigestion.

—DOROTHY PARKER ON MARION DAVIES

He liked to be the biggest bug on the manure pile.

—ELIA KAZAN ON HARRY COHN, STUDIO MOGUL

When everybody is somebody, then no one's anybody.

—W. S. GILBERT

Nothing is so commonplace as to wish to be remarkable.

—OLIVER WENDELL HOLMES

When Theodore attends a wedding, he wants to be the bride, and when he attends a funeral, he wants to be the corpse.

—ALICE ROOSEVELT LONGWORTH ON THEODORE ROOSEVELT

The nice thing about being a celebrity is that when you bore people, they think it's their fault.

—HENRY KISSINGER

Like most censors he was perfectly convinced that his own tastes were somehow in tune with the music of the spheres . . . behind his complacency lay the assumption of a Deity who had chosen to infuse into the Best People a practically infallible sense of what was right, what wrong.

—E. M. HALLIDAY ON THOMAS BOWDLER

A painter paints his pictures on canvas. But musicians paint their pictures on silence. We provide the music, and you provide the silence!

—LEOPOLD STOKOWSKI (REPRIMANDING A TALKATIVE AUDIENCE)

*If one hears bad music it is one's duty to drown it out
by one's conversation.*

—OSCAR WILDE

We are not amused.

—QUEEN VICTORIA

*No two men ever judged alike of the same thing, and it
is impossible to find two opinions exactly similar, not only
in different men but in the same men at different times.*

—MICHEL DE MONTAIGNE

*I have found through my experiences that critics know
what you're thinking or trying to portray as much as a baby in
Afghanistan would understand when you speak English.*

—DIZZY GILLESPIE

No statue has ever been put up to a critic.

—JEAN SIBELIUS

Having the critics praise you is like having the hangman
say you've got a pretty neck.

—ELI WALLACH

Of making many books there is no end . . .

—ECCLESIASTES 12:12 (RSV)

Sometimes even good old Homer nods.

—HORACE

This paperback is very interesting,
but I find it will never replace a hardcover book—
it makes a very poor doorstop.

—ALFRED HITCHCOCK

Author: a fool who, not content with having bored those
who have lived with him, insists on tormenting
the generations to come.

—MONTESQUIEU

Never judge a book by its movie.

—J. W. EAGAN

Beware of allowing a tactless word, a rebuttal, a rejection
to obliterate the whole sky.

—ANAÏS NIN

Two of the cruelest, most primitive punishments our town deals out . . .
are the empty mailbox and the silent telephone.

—HEDDA HOPPER

Failure is the foundation of success, and the means
by which it is achieved. Success is the lurking-place of failure;
but who can tell when the turning point will come?

—LAO-TSE

The musical experience needs three human beings at least.
It requires a composer, a performer, and a listener; and unless
these three take part together there is no musical experience.

—BENJAMIN BRITTEN

When Stravinsky's ballet *The Rite of Spring* was first performed
in Paris in 1913, the audience, shocked by the dissonant
and "barbarous" music, rioted.

Give me the best instrument in Europe,
but listeners who understand nothing or do not wish to understand
and who do not feel with me in what I am playing,
and all my pleasure is spoiled.

—WOLFGANG AMADEUS MOZART

A really great reception makes me feel like I have a
great big warm heating pad all over me.
I truly have a great love for an audience.

—JUDY GARLAND

A [Judy Garland] audience doesn't just listen.
They have their arms around her when she works.

—SPENCER TRACY

Art and Heart

Though critics may bow to art, and I am its own true lover,
It is not art, but heart, which wins the wide world over.

Though smooth be the heartless prayer, no ear in Heaven will mind it,
And the finest phrase falls dead, if there is no feeling behind it.

Though perfect the player's touch, little if any he sways us,
Unless we feel his heart throb through the music he plays us.

Though the poet may spend his life in skillfully rounding a measure,
Unless he writes from a full warm heart, he gives us little pleasure.

So it is not the speech which tells, but the impulse which goes with the saying,
And it is not the words of the prayer, but the yearning back of the praying.

It is not the artist's skill, which into our soul comes stealing
With a joy that is almost pain, but it is the player's feeling.

And it is not the poet's song, though sweeter than sweet bells chiming,
Which thrills us through and through, but the heart which beats under the
rhyming.

And therefore I say again, though I am art's own true lover,
That it is not art, but heart, which wins the wide world over.

—ELLA WHEELER WILCOX

The Poet and His Songs

As the birds come in Spring,
We know not from where,
As the stars come at evening
From the depths of the air;

As the rain comes from the cloud,
And the brook from the ground;
As suddenly, low or loud,
Out of silence a sound;

As the grape comes to the vine,
The fruit to the tree;
As the wind comes to the pine,
And the tide to the sea;

As come the white sails of ships
O'er the ocean's verge;
As comes the smile to the lips,
The foam to the surge;

So come to the Poet his songs,
All hitherward blown
From the misty realm that belongs
To the vast unknown.

His, and not his, are the lays
He sings; and their fame
Is his, and not his; and the praise
And the pride of a name.

For voices pursue him by day
And haunt him by night,
And he listens and needs must obey,
When the Angel says, "Write!"
—HENRY WADSWORTH LONGFELLOW

The Art of Encouragement

I produce music as an apple tree produces apples.
—CAMILLE SAINT-SAËNS

From the heart, may it again go to the heart.
—LUDWIG VAN BEETHOVEN

When I play, I make love—it is the same thing.
—ARTUR RUBINSTEIN

With cries of labor I gave birth to this hymn.
—ENHEDUANNA

I am in the world only for the purpose of composing.
What I feel in my heart, I give to the world.
—FRANZ SCHUBERT

Can that which has cost the artists days, weeks, months,
and even years of reflection be understood in a flash by the dilettante?
—ROBERT SCHUMANN

The Winds of Fate

One ship drives east and another drives west,
With the self-same winds that blow,
        'Tis the set of the sails
        And not the gales
That tell them the way to go.

Like the winds of the sea are the winds of fate,
As we voyage along through life,
        'Tis the set of the soul
        That decides its goal
And not the calm or the strife.
—ELLA WHEELER WILCOX

The contrary winds may blow strong in my face,
    yet I will go forward and never turn back.
    —TEEDYUSCUNG, LEADER OF THE LENAPE PEOPLE

Encouraging Each Other

I am the mate and companion of all people, all just as
immortal and fathomless as myself;
(They do not know how immortal, but I know.)

—WALT WHITMAN

PILGRIM SOULS ON THE PATH TOGETHER

Your neighbor is your other self dwelling behind a wall.
In understanding, all walls fall down.

—KAHLIL GIBRAN

Reveal the golden treasure of yourself to the world. Discover the golden treasure of others in the world. Look into another's eyes and see a reflection of yourself. Look into your heart and see the stranger gazing back, waiting for your response. Train yourself in goodness, honor your individuality. And so you may honor and appreciate the goodness and individuality of others.

We are not meant to stand alone, or be all unto ourselves. We are meant for each other. It is not easy, but it is worthwhile, this pilgrimage to find the *other* and then to discover our reflection in the face of one who may seem on the surface to be vastly different from ourselves. Anything worthwhile takes hard, hard work and long years of love and discipline that grow sweeter as time passes. The discipline of love, the heart that is open, is the greatest pilgrimage of all.

You start by learning to listen to your own voice. But it does not end with you. This is preparation to hear the voices of others, each as unique as you, with the same desire for love, the same need for healing, the same search for meaning. During the first part of the pilgrimage, you walk through a desert alone and learn the tender terror of a solitude that stills you and enables you to listen to God. And then you discover that you have the power to recognize in others the voice of God that you heard during your desert seclusion.

Encouragement is ultimately the gift of discovering the beauty of each person's precious treasure of individuality. It is training yourself in the art of love, then taking those lessons out into the world. You train yourself to see with the eyes of love, to appreciate with a heart of gratitude, and to extend a hand to help others perceive that they are loved, they are unique, and they have gifts to offer the world. If solitude is the sound of one hand clapping, then applause is the joining of many hands in a circle of giving and appreciation.

Our task is to learn that if we can voyage to the ends of the earth and find ourselves in the aborigine who most differs from ourselves, we will have made a fruitful pilgrimage. That is why pilgrimage is necessary, in some shape or other.

—THOMAS MERTON

I admit that this vision of seeing the other as ourselves can seem more like an idealistic dream than a living reality. When some guy talking on his cell phone cuts you off in traffic, or your kids whine one too many times in an afternoon, or your boss makes an unfair decision, or your mate forgets something that is important to you, it's hard to see the beauty in every person. What you'd really like to do is have some moral policeman hand them a ticket for bad behavior. In the daily world, we get jostled and our toes get stepped on. Desert solitude sounds pretty good after a hectic day at the office.

Yes, there is pain, rejection, and heartache. But if we choose a contained solitude or a circle of exclusivity, life is no safer in the end. It is, in fact, far more dangerous. We are meant to grow and learn from each other. We are meant to nurture our souls in the traffic of the great wide world, as well as in the private gardens of family and intimate friendship.

One lighted torch serves to light another.

—FREDERICK GODET

As iron sharpens iron, so one man sharpens another.
—PROVERBS 27:17 (NIV)

If not now, when?
—MARTIN BUBER

If not you, then who? You have to start somewhere, believe something. *You* are the answer to the world's question. Your gifts are to be shaped on the anvil of life and fired in the furnace of adversity, so that they can be polished to reflect the light of shared experience. You do not have to be a superhero; you can choose to start with the work at hand.

It begins with you. Value yourself. Then value others. The quiet contagion of example can spread. It will make a difference, one person at a time. If each of us chooses to make even a small difference in our corner of the universe, then perhaps we can be part of a movement that could one day transform the world. Idealistic? You bet. And isn't it a relief to be idealistic and give free rein to our highest dreams? To choose to practice the art of encouragement is to invest in your best and most idealistic dreams.

We become just by performing just actions,
temperate by performing temperate actions,
brave by performing brave actions.
—ARISTOTLE

Everything that lives, lives not alone, nor for itself.
—WILLIAM BLAKE

Let me tell you why you are here. You're here to be salt-seasoning that brings out the God-flavors of this earth. If you lose your saltiness, how will people taste godliness? You've lost your usefulness and will end up in the garbage. Here's another way to put it: You're here to be light, bringing out the God-colors in the world. God is not a secret to be kept. We're going public with this, as public as a city on a hill. If I make you light-bearers, you don't think I'm going to hide you under a bucket, do you? I'm putting you on a light stand. Now that I've put you there on a hilltop, on a light stand—shine! Keep open house; be generous with your lives. By opening up to others, you'll prompt people to open up with God, this generous Father in heaven.
—MATTHEW 5: 13-16 (THE MESSAGE)

Let God love you through others and let
God love others through you.

—D. M. STREET

I sought to hear the voice of God
And climbed the topmost steeple,
But God declared: "Go down again—
I dwell among the people."

—JOHN HENRY NEWMAN

If I speak in the tongues of men and of angels,
but have not love, I am a noisy gong or a clanging cymbal.
And if I have prophetic powers, and understand all mysteries and
all knowledge, and if I have all faith, so as to remove mountains,
but have not love, I am nothing. If I give away all I have, and if I
deliver my body to be burned, but have not love, I gain nothing.

—I CORINTHIANS 13:1–3 (RSV)

Any old woman can love God better than a doctor of theology can.

—SAINT BONAVENTURE

So long as we love, we serve. So long as we are loved by others,
I would almost say we are indispensable;
and no man is useless when he has a friend.

—ROBERT LOUIS STEVENSON

Tell me whom you love, and I will tell you what you are.

—ARSÈNE HOUSSAYE

A man is not where he lives, but where he loves.

—LATIN PROVERB

A good man, through obscurest aspirations,
Has still an instinct of the one true way.

—GOETHE

Selfishness is the only real atheism; aspiration, the only real religion.

—ISRAEL ZANGWILL

God likes help when helping people.

—IRISH PROVERB

He has achieved success who has lived well,
laughed often, and loved much.

—BESSIE ANDERSON STANLEY

Jesus throws down the dividing prejudices of nationality,
and teaches universal love, without distinction of race,
merit, or rank. A man's neighbor is everyone that needs help.

—JOHN CUNNINGHAM GEIKIE

One man gives freely, yet grows all the richer;
another withholds what he should give and only suffers want.
A liberal man will be enriched,
and one who waters will himself be watered.

—PROVERBS 11:24–25 (RSV)

The universe is but one great city, full of beloved ones,
divine and human by nature, endeared to each other.
—EPICTETUS

Rejoice with them that do rejoice, and weep with them that weep.
—ROMANS 12:15 (KJV)

We are members of one great body, planted by nature in
a mutual love, and fitted for a social life. We must consider
that we were born for the good of the whole.
—SENECA

Our modern industrialized society is a good deal
like the subway—it throws men together in physical proximity
without uniting them in spiritual sympathy.
—HARRY EMERSON FOSDICK

Keep your heart with all diligence; for out of it are the issues of life.
—PROVERBS 4:23 (KJV)

Encouraging Each Other

Teach me to feel another's woe,
To hide the fault I see:
That mercy I to others show,
That mercy show to me.
—ALEXANDER POPE

There is much satisfaction in work well done; praise is sweet; but there can be no
happiness equal to the joy of finding a heart that understands.
—VICTOR ROBINSOLL

Two men please God—who serves Him with all his heart because he knows Him;
who seeks Him with all his heart because he knows Him not.
—NIKITA IVANOVICH PANIN

There can be no peace on earth until we have learned to respect the dignity of man
and are willing to build on the foundation of human love the kind of world
that the great teachers of mankind have portrayed to us from the time of the
Ten Commandments and Sermon on the Mount.
—DAVID LAWRENCE

The world is now too dangerous for anything but the truth,
too small for anything but brotherhood.
—ADLAI STEVENSON

Love is the crowning grace of humanity, the holiest right of the soul, the golden
link which binds us to duty and truth, the redeeming principle that chiefly
reconciles the heart of life, and is prophetic of eternal good.
—PETRARCH

Love is an image of God, and not a lifeless image, but the living essence of
the divine nature which beams full of all goodness.
—MARTIN LUTHER

A pennyweight o' love is worth a pound o' law.
—SCOTTISH PROVERB

Paradise is open to all good hearts.
—PIERRE JEAN DE BÉRANGER

Whoever gives a small coin to a poor man has six blessings bestowed upon him,
but he who speaks a kind word to him obtains eleven blessings.

—THE TALMUD

The heart of a good man is the sanctuary of God in this world.

—MADAME NECKER

The Lord showed me, so that I did see clearly,
that he did not dwell in these temples
which men had commanded and set up,
but in people's hearts.

—GEORGE FOX

O brother man, fold to thy heart thy brother;
Where pity dwells, the peace of God is there;
To worship rightly is to love each other,
Each smile a hymn, each kindly deed a prayer.

—JOHN GREENLEAF WHITTIER

COMPASSION

Success is to be measured not so much by the
position that one has reached in life as by the obstacles
which he has overcome while trying to succeed.
—BOOKER T. WASHINGTON

Have compassion and empathy for others. See what they are trying to accomplish. Appreciate their efforts. Understand the obstacles they may be trying to overcome. Be aware of our mutual mortality and humanity.

I am convinced that everyone is a hidden hero. If you know a person's story, you might be surprised by the courage and grace displayed in difficult circumstances. I am continually amazed when I listen to people tell me the important stories of their lives—those crucial choices they had to make during hard times. One of the earthiest and most loving women I know was in a car accident with her parents. A drunk driver hit them at an intersection, and her mother and father were killed instantly. She survived, but it was months before she recovered from her injuries. Yet this woman is not bitter. Her tender heart expresses itself instead in compassion for others. Her warm home is a sanctuary for healing.

I know other hidden heroes, too. A woman who was raped as a teenager now shares her journey of growth and healing with those who seek solace at a rape crisis center. A man works hard to take care of his wife and children, faithfully doing his job even when it proves difficult. Artists and songwriters hold day jobs and do their creative work in their spare time until the big break comes along. People quietly make a difference in the lives of others through volunteer activities and acts of compassion that no eye sees but the eye of God. There are so many people whose stories are dramas of incredible heroism—yet they would never call themselves heroes.

A good parent encourages a child and is aware that developing minds and bodies can accomplish certain tasks at a certain age. So you can be aware that we are all at different points of growth in our soul-life here on earth. Each person is learning a different lesson. Lessons that are easy for you may be a struggle for someone else. Lessons that come easily to others may be like giant fire-breathing dragons to you. Everyone's struggle is unique, but we can learn from one another's struggles. We need to open our hearts to appreciate what each person has survived and overcome.

Look for the hidden heroism in the lives of others. Ask yourself: Did this person come from a broken home? Is she recovering from an abusive relationship? Has that person faced a personal tragedy? Is he a sensitive person with an artistic bent who was ridiculed for not being more "manly"? Did she feel like an ugly duckling when she was growing up, and is only now discovering her inner beauty? Has he just been working through a crisis or grieving a loss?

Gifts and talents can bring with them a need for hidden heroism. Did this person's combination of gifts and talents come with an overly sensitive temperament? Is this person a quiet late bloomer, ignored by a society that values early, spectacular blossoms? Is this a person who had success at a young age, and now has to learn lessons of humility and self-reinvention? Is this a complex person who is difficult to label and pigeonhole—and therefore has had trouble fitting in with the school system, the specialization of the workplace, or the popular agenda of the crowd?

Give people credit for the obstacles they have overcome to get to where they are now. Give yourself credit for your efforts. Look at your childhood, your family, your circumstances, your potential, and your limitations. Look at them with the eyes of mercy and compassion instead of judgment and regret. Be compassionate to yourself and to others.

You did the best you could with what you had at the time. Do not beat yourself up for being human. Accept the good and the bad. Remove emotional judgment and see clearly the obstacles and difficulties you have overcome to bring you to this place.

Allow compassion and forgiveness to color the lens through which you view your life and the lives of others. A perspective based in gentle empathy and nonjudgmental awareness helps you see yourself—and others—in a new light.

If you want to see virtue,
you have to have a calm mind.
—SHUNRYU SUZUKI ROSHI

Flops are a part of life's menu,
and I've never been a girl to miss out on any of the courses.
—JANE RUSSELL

There are defeats more triumphant than victories.
—MICHEL DE MONTAIGNE

The Art of Encouragement

I thank God for my handicaps for, through them,
I have found myself, my work, and my God.
—HELEN KELLER

I looked more widely around me,
I studied the lives of the masses of humanity, and I saw that,
not two or three, or ten, but hundreds, thousands, millions,
had so understood the meaning of life that they were able
both to live and to die. All these men were well acquainted
with the meaning of life and death, quietly labored,
endured privation and suffering, lived and died,
and saw in all this, not a vain, but a good thing.
—LEO TOLSTOY

God himself, sir, does not propose to judge a man until
his life is over. Why should you and I?
—SAMUEL JOHNSON

He has the right to criticize who has the heart to help.
—ABRAHAM LINCOLN

Making Life Worthwhile

Every soul that touches yours—
Be it the slightest contact—
Gets therefrom some good;
Some little grace; one kindly thought;
One aspiration yet unfelt;
One bit of courage
For the darkening sky;
One gleam of faith
To brave the thickening ills of life;
One glimpse of brighter skies—
To make this life worthwhile
And heaven a surer heritage.

—GEORGE ELIOT

RELATING TO ONE ANOTHER

Suppose you scrub your ethical skin until it shines,
but inside there is no music. Then what?

—KABIR

Relationships are complex. There are no easy answers or formulas to create the perfect relationship—or the perfect person. But sometimes it helps if we can ask ourselves the right questions when we are trying to find more effective ways to relate to one another. Here are a few ideas, questions, and suggestions for dealing wisely with one another and living from our hearts as well as our heads.

When a man's ways are pleasing to the Lord,
he makes even his enemies live at peace with him.

—PROVERBS 16:7 (NIV)

He who wishes to secure the good of
others has already secured his own.
—CONFUCIUS

If you've gotten anything at all out of following Christ,
if his love has made any difference in your life,
if being in a community of the spirit means anything to you,
if you have a heart, if you care—then do me a favor:
Agree with each other, love each other, be deep-spirited friends.
Don't push your way to the front;
don't sweet-talk your way to the top.
Put yourself aside, and help others get ahead.
Don't be obsessed with getting your own advantage.
Forget yourselves long enough to lend a helping hand.
—PHILIPPIANS 2:1–4 (THE MESSAGE)

Saints are what they are not because of their sanctity
but because the gift of sainthood makes it possible
for them to admire everyone else.
—THOMAS MERTON

BE CLEAR ABOUT YOUR DEEPEST MOTIVES.

Know your own heart and be willing to face your own truths before you demand it of others. Make a conscious choice to choose the best, and understand that it is easy to fool yourself. Be as honest as you can be and stand for what you believe in. As trainers advise steeplechase jockeys about jumping fences, pick your panel and stick with it. Express who you really are rather than playing a part to please or impress others.

This above all: to thine own self be true,
And it must follow, as the night the day,
Thou canst not then be false to any man.
—WILLIAM SHAKESPEARE

A man without a high purpose is like a ship without a rudder
—a waif, a nothing, a no man.
—THOMAS CARLYLE

What good is it for a man to gain the whole world,
yet forfeit his soul?
—MARK 8:36 (NIV)

Act with determination not to be turned aside
by thoughts of the past and fears of the future.
—ROBERT E. LEE

Resolve to be thyself, and know that he who finds himself, loses his misery.
—COVENTRY PATMORE

WALK YOUR TALK.

Does what you do match up with what you say you believe? Do you believe in a forgiving God, yet judge others harshly? Do you say you hate gossip, but rejoice when you hear of someone else's downfall? Are you contemptuous of certain kinds of people, yet proud of your own moral superiority? Are you courageous enough to do what needs to be done, no matter what the cost?

It is more important to understand
the ground of your own behavior than to
understand the motives of another.
—DAG HAMMARSKJÖLD

Character is what you are in the dark.

—DWIGHT L. MOODY

*A man is already of consequence in the world
when it is known that we can implicitly rely upon him.
Often I have known a man to be preferred in
stations of honour and profit because he had this reputation:
when he said he knew a thing, he knew it,
and when he said he would do a thing, he did it.*

—EDWARD BULWER-LYTTON

*And since you know that he cares, let your language show it.
Don't add words like "I swear to God" to your own words.
Don't show your impatience by concocting oaths to hurry up God.
Just say yes or no. Just say what is true. That way, your language
can't be used against you.*

—JAMES 5:12 (THE MESSAGE)

TRUST THE PROCESS.

Surrender to the wisdom of life. Your ego wants to control the process and have an assured end product. But when you honor the wisdom of your own process, you can discover your unique path to creative freedom. Be willing to live with the questions for a while instead of demanding instant answers. Know that each choice you make is a step in the right direction, even when you don't know where you're going. Trusting the process in your life helps you allow others to go through their own process, trusting that their soul's journey is as valid as yours. Know that mistakes, failures, and detours are just as much a part of the process as successes and accomplishments. The universe has its own timing that must be respected.

We go all wrong by too strenuous a resolution to go all right.
—NATHANIEL HAWTHORNE

If you follow your bliss, you put yourself on a kind of track,
which has been there all the while waiting for you,
and the life that you ought to be living is the one you are living.
—JOSEPH CAMPBELL

Everything comes to us that belongs to us
if we create the capacity to receive it.
—RABINDRANATH TAGORE

The work of art is above all a process of creation,
it is never experienced as a mere product.
—PAUL KLEE

The artist does not see things as they are, but as he is.
—ALFRED TONNELLE

Artists in each of the arts seek after
and care for nothing but love.
—MARSILIO FICINO

If we are able to stay with a situation,
it will carry us to a new place.
—SHAUN MCNIFF

There is no road too long to the man who advances deliberately
and without undue haste; no honors too distant to the man
who prepares himself for them with patience.

—JEAN DE LA BRUYÈRE

Thousands of people have talent.
I might as well congratulate you for having eyes in your head.
The one and only thing that counts is:
Do you have staying power?

—NOEL COWARD

RESPECT YOURSELF AND OTHERS.

God created and it was good, it says in Genesis. Do you look in the mirror and see someone who reflects the sacredness of all creation? Have you taken time to see the goodness of God in others? Honor every person as one who is loved by God and worthy of your respect. No matter how flawed we are, there is a sacred flame that burns in each of our hearts. Do not quench that flame with disrespect. Respect the fact that all of life is sacred, a mystery to be celebrated.

How far you go in life depends on your
being tender with the young, compassionate with the aged,
sympathetic with the striving, and tolerant of the weak
and the strong. Because someday in life
you will have been all of these.
—GEORGE WASHINGTON CARVER

Be kind, everyone you meet is fighting a hard battle.
—JOHN WATSON

STAY CENTERED AND KEEP YOUR BALANCE.

What does it mean to stay centered? In some ways, it is like the elegant balance of a ballerina. For every moment she is on stage performing, she has spent hours stretching and strengthening her muscles, learning to listen to and know her own body.

In the same way, you can train yourself to be an athlete of the spirit, by listening to your heart and feeling the inner equilibrium. Little by little, you learn to know when you are pushing too hard, pulling back too much, or moving with grace and freedom. Simple exercises of grace can help you develop spiritual strength and coordination:

- ❖ reading spiritual books
- ❖ performing small acts of kindness
- ❖ choosing to believe the best in each situation
- ❖ taking time for meditation and stillness
- ❖ writing in a journal
- ❖ walking
- ❖ exploring spiritual disciplines and exercises
- ❖ allowing things to be as they are, rather than pushing to make them conform to your agenda
- ❖ living in the moment, instead of worrying about the future or hashing over the past
- ❖ practicing gratitude and delight, instead of complaining and worrying

As you find your own balance, you will find it easier to be centered in your relationships with others. Your giving will be more sensitive. You will intuitively know how to minister to hidden needs instead of just trying to solve an outer problem. You won't give too much too soon, which can overwhelm and overload the receiver. And you won't give too little, too late, either. Staying centered helps you give for the right reasons—instead of being motivated by guilt or shame—in a way that is appropriate to the other person's need. A continuous flow of help is available to all of us. If you are centered, you are able to receive from that flow as well as give to it. Sometimes your willingness to receive is the greatest gift of all, for the ego's pride is set aside to make you an equal with another, instead of claiming superiority over someone else. Be willing to accept help when you need it. Offer help when you feel moved to give it.

SPEAK WITH VISION, CLARITY, AND KINDNESS.

Be positive. Instead of concentrating on the problem, look for the solution. Focus on the good, the true, the beautiful. Look for possibilities and see the potential in each person, each situation. Focused for good, your positive energy has great power.

Tell the truth. Say what you mean instead of making easy promises that mean nothing. Keep your word. Be kind and generous. Let your language be filled with loving words instead of critical judgment.

Encouraging Each Other

Once you have spoken, even the swiftest horse cannot retract your words.

—CHINESE PROVERB

*Words can destroy. What we call each other ultimately
becomes what we think of each other, and it matters.*

—JEANNE J. KIRKPATRICK

*A wise man's heart guides his mouth,
and his lips promote instruction.
Pleasant words are a honeycomb,
sweet to the soul and healing to the bones.*

—PROVERBS 16:25–26 (NIV)

What is lofty can be said in any language. What is mean should be said in none.

—MAIMONIDES

*My life is an indivisible whole,
and all my activities run into one another;
and they have their rise in my insatiable love of mankind.*

—MAHATMA GANDHI

161

Thoughts rule the world.

—RALPH WALDO EMERSON

As water reflects a face, so a man's heart reflects the man.

—PROVERBS 27:19 (NIV)

BE OPEN TO HELP FROM UNEXPECTED SOURCES.

When you ask God for help, resources, and guidance, visualize the end result. But leave the *how* up to God. The universe is a complex and mysterious place and our minds too finite to comprehend all the ways God can meet our needs. I have found that when I think a situation is going to work itself out a certain way, it's almost certain that it will work out in an unexpected way and on a different schedule than I had anticipated. God loves to surprise us. And He loves to provide for us—if we'll just get out of the road and allow him to do it His own way.

Today I live in the quiet joyous expectation of good.

—ERNEST HOLMES

Life is a series of surprises.

—RALPH WALDO EMERSON

As the heavens are higher than the earth,
so are my ways higher than your ways and
my thoughts than your thoughts.

—ISAIAH 55:9 (NIV)

Many people pray and receive the answer to their prayers,
but ignore them—or deny them, because the answers didn't
come in the expected form.

—SOPHY BURNHAM

LISTEN

The greatest gift we can give one another is
rapt attention to one another's existence.

—SUE ATCHLEY EBAUGH

Listen. Do you take the time to stop and really listen? Are you listening to others? Are you listening to the sounds of life around you? Are you listening to your own life? Do you allow God to get a word in edgewise—or are you too busy trying to manipulate circumstances and dictate terms? Are you willing to be quiet and listen long enough to hear your deepest truths, from the sacred center of your heart? Are you willing to take the time to listen without judgment and to wait for communion from heart to heart?

We live in a culture that loves diagnosis, quick fixes, and cure-alls. We want to name the disease, pigeonhole the problem, and get on with our agenda. Looking for instant answers, we love the convenient cure, the magic bullet, the bottle of medicine that will get rid of the symptoms, even if it does not heal the disease.

We want productivity and efficiency, not personal communion and the messiness of community living. We want conforming consumers, not complicated people in their complex matrix of joy and sorrow, dreams and disappointments. "Hurry! Hurry! Fix this person! Get rid of this heartache! Let us get on with our busy agenda and cross this off our list as a project completed." We do this not only to others, but to ourselves as well.

Why? Why do we measure our lives and our worth and our time on such a small scale? Why are we so ungenerous with ourselves, stingy with our hearts? Why do we try to fill the emptiness with possessions and medicate our sorrows with money, prestige, and eternal busyness? Why do we constantly fill our ears with noise and our lives with speed, leaving no time for those we love? Day after day, our oppressive schedules and mechanistic expectations drain yet another increment of joy from our souls. We rush from task to task, feeling guilty if we take any time for ourselves or for simple listening. We are tired from this hectic pace. We need to retreat into a time of rest and silence. Only then will we be prepared to really hear our own thoughts and to listen as others speak their hearts to us.

We are not meant to produce continually. We are not efficient machines that just need some tinkering. We are organic beings, requiring nurture and rest. We need time to think, time to sleep. We need to move with the natural rhythms of our biology, to rest beside still waters, and to listen.

Before we can truly listen to others, we must begin to listen to ourselves, and listening takes time. This is not a project to be accomplished with a day's hard work; it takes a lifetime of cultivating openness and patience.

Listening to yourself begins with a few quiet, honest minutes. It begins with one small choice—to give yourself permission to stop and to listen, to say to yourself, "I will take small breaks in my day to be quiet. I will honor my humanity, rest my busy mind, and listen to the rhythm of my heart."

Your heart knows the truth and, if you slow down long enough, it will tell you what you need to know. You will know whether your life is busy because it is fulfilling—or because you are trying to avoid your deepest truth. Your heart is good, and you are good. But you will not know this if you will not take the time to listen, to allow your heart to speak its wisdom to you. When you can listen to your own truths, then you will not be afraid of the truths others hold in their hearts.

When you learn to listen, you will be able to be a true friend. Instead of thinking of others as disposable objects or pawns to move about on the chessboard of your life, you will see that they are sacred and precious. You will discover that, when you take the time to listen to them, you will hear echoes of your own heart's cries. You will also hear the voice of God calling to you through their voices and the voice of creation. Your friendships will deepen and become more real because you have learned to listen from the heart, instead of allowing your mind to constantly interrupt and criticize.

Your time and attention are the greatest gifts you have to offer—one sacred being to another, listening and laughing and crying and caring—heart-to-heart communion instead of merely communicating information.

Your time and attention are also gifts to offer to God. If you don't take time out for listening, healing, and nurturing yourself and others, you will find that life will find a way to take you out of your busyness—through illness or crisis. So take a walk in the quiet. Spend time with friends and loved ones. In every day, every moment, God is whispering to us, if we have the ears to hear. Listen.

Listen, my children, with the ear of your heart.
—SAINT BENEDICT

He maketh me to lie down in green pastures: he leadeth me beside
still waters. He restoreth my soul.
—PSALM 23:2–3 (KJV)

There are unknown forces within nature;
when we give ourselves wholly to her, without reserve,
she leads them to us; she shows us those forms
which our watching eyes do not see,
which our intelligence does not understand or suspect.

—AUGUSTE RODIN

Absolute unmixed attention is prayer.

—SIMONE WEIL

All things and all men, so to speak, call on us
with small or loud voices. They want us to listen.
They want us to understand their intrinsic claims,
their justice of being. But we can give it to them
only through the love that listens.

—PAUL TILLICH

Listening, not imitation, may be the sincerest form of flattery.

—DR. JOYCE BROTHERS

Oh the comfort, the inexpressible comfort of feeling safe with
a person; having neither to weigh thoughts nor to measure words
but to pour them all out, just as it is, chaff and grain together, knowing
that a faithful hand will take and sift them, keeping what is worth keeping,
and then, with the breath of kindness, blow the rest away.

—GEORGE ELIOT

How can we communicate love? I think three things are involved:
We must reach out to a person, make contact.
We must listen with the heart, be sensitive to the other's needs.
We must respond in a language that the person can understand.
Many of us do all the talking.
We must learn to listen and to keep on listening.

—PRINCESS PALE MOON

True friendship comes when silence between two people is comfortable.

—DAVE TYSON GENTRY

If you want to be listened to, you should put in time listening.

—MARGE PIERCY

Holy listening—to "listen" another's soul into life,
into a condition of disclosure and discovery,
may be almost the greatest service that
any human being ever performs for another.
—DOUGLAS STEERE

The real art of conversation is not only to
say the right thing in the right place but to leave unsaid
the wrong thing at the tempting moment.
—LADY DOROTHY NEVILL

We have all known the long loneliness and we have learned that
the only solution is love and that love comes with community.
—DOROTHY DAY

Be gracious in your speech.
The goal is to bring out the best in others in a conversation,
not put them down, cut them down.
—COLOSSIANS 4:6 (THE MESSAGE)

The most called-upon prerequisite of a friend is an accessible ear.

—MAYA ANGELOU

Most of our misfortunes are comments of our friends upon them.

—CHARLES CALEB COLTON

Many argue; not many converse.

—LOUISA MAY ALCOTT

Treat your friends as you do your best pictures, and place them in their best light.

—JENNIE JEROME CHURCHILL

In friendship, let there be laughter and sharing of pleasures.

—KAHLIL GIBRAN

We take care of our health, we lay up money, we make our room tight, and our clothing sufficient; but who provides wisely that he shall not be wanting in the best property of all—friends?

—RALPH WALDO EMERSON

.

A friend is a present you give yourself.

—ROBERT LOUIS STEVENSON

Keep some opinions to yourself. Say what you please of others, but never repeat what you hear said of them to themselves. If you have nothing to offer yourself, laugh with the witty, assent to the wise; they will not think the worse of you for it. Listen to information on subjects you are unacquainted with, instead of always striving to lead the conversation to some favourite one of your own. By the last method you will shine, but not improve. I am ashamed myself ever to open my lips on any question I have ever written upon.

—WILLIAM HAZLITT

Listen carefully to what country people call mother wit. In those homely sayings are couched the collective wisdom of generations.

—MAYA ANGELOU

Hold fast to the words of your ancestors.

—HOPI PROVERB

*Bend from the lofty perch of your own disciplines
and listen with regard to disciplines not your own.
If you are an engineer, listen to the artist; if you are a physicist,
listen to the philosopher; if you are a logician,
listen to the religionist; and especially if you are
in a position of power, listen, listen.*

—CHAIM POTOK

*Everyone should be quick to listen, slow to speak, slow to become angry,
for man's anger does not bring about the righteous life God desires.*

JAMES 1:19-20 (NIV)

Silences make the real conversation between friends.

—MARGARET LEE RUNBECK

*When a woman is speaking to you,
listen to what she says with her eyes.*

—VICTOR HUGO

Encouraging Our World

Glance at the sun.
See the moon and stars.
Gaze at the beauty of
the Earth's greenings.
Now think.

—SAINT HILDEGARD VON BINGEN

THE WAY OF BLESSING

Before me, may it be beautiful.
Behind me, may it be beautiful.
Around me, may it be beautiful.
Below me, may it be beautiful.
Above me, may it be beautiful.
All, may it be beautiful.

—NAVAJO PRAYER

I used to work at a very large, well-stocked Christian bookstore. Though I managed the music department, I loved browsing in the biblical reference section. I loved the encyclopedias, commentaries, archeological histories, and books on customs and cultures of Bible times. But one of my favorite resources was the section on word studies. The shelf was filled with all kinds of wonderful books that went back to the original Greek, Hebrew, or Aramaic and offered insights and backgrounds on the meaning of words found in the Bible.

Look in any good dictionary and you will find the history of a word—how it developed in the language and how its meaning changed and expanded through the years. For instance, the root of the word *encouragement* is *coeur*, which is French for *heart*. When I meditate on the meanings that flow from the heart, *encouragement* becomes a richer word for me. Understanding a word, its meaning and its history, can open the mind to larger ideas and the heart to new meaning—especially if that definition has crossed through more than one culture.

Howard Rheingold, in his book *They Have a Word for It: A Lighthearted Lexicon of Untranslatable Words and Phrases*, says, "Thinking about the right kind of untranslatable words creates a certain state of mind. I found myself looking at the mundane elements of everyday life through a new kind of lens, which revealed to me dimensions in my familiar environment that I had simply not seen before because I hadn't known how to look." A new word—or a new idea—can offer us a different perspective on the attitudes and thoughts we live with habitually.

Linguist Benjamin Lee Whorf writes, "We dissect nature along lines laid down by our native languages. . . . We cut nature up, organize it into concepts, and ascribe significances as we do, largely because we are parties to an agreement to organize it this way—an agreement that holds throughout our speech community and is codified in the patterns of our language." Whorf's book *Language, Thought, and Reality* offers what has come to be known as the Whorfian hypothesis. This theory says that differences in language actually affect our perception of reality and cause us to think differently because we organize information differently. Rheingold says, "Finding a name for something is a way of conjuring its existence, of making it possible for people to see a pattern where they didn't see anything before."

I would like to use the word *blessing* to conjure a new pattern for our relationship to one another. It's an ancient idea that is especially meaningful for our time and culture. Blessing offers a lens for seeing our world in a new way, expanding the boundaries of our ideas and reaching deep into our hearts. It can be a pattern for how we live in our world—*being* a blessing as well as giving or receiving a blessing.

Blessing is "the act of declaring, or wishing, favor and goodness upon others," according to Nelson's *New Illustrated Bible Dictionary*. "The blessing is not only the good effect of words; it also has the power to bring them to pass." There are several forms of the word *bless* in the Bible, for example, the Hebrew word *barach*, which means "to bless, to salute, to congratulate, to thank, to praise, or to kneel down." The root of the word contains pictures of bending the knee, and can also mean *pool*. It is closely related to *bara*, the word for *create*. And with the change of one vowel, the word can denote camels kneeling at an oasis pool in a dry desert.

A New Testament Greek form of the word is *eulogeo*, from *eu—well* or *good—* and *logos—speech* or *word*. Our English word *eulogy* is related to *eulogeo*, which means "to speak well of, praise, extol, bless abundantly, invoke a benediction, and give thanks." The Old English word *bless* stems from the Teutonic word *blod* (blood) and, according to the Oxford English Dictionary, was originally used to refer to marking or consecrating with blood. But the word was chosen at its conversion into English to render the Latin word *benedicere*, "to praise," from which we get the word *benediction*.

Matthew Fox, in his book *Original Blessing*, says, "Blessing involves relationship: one does not bless without investing something of oneself into the receiver of one's blessing. . . . A theology of blessing is a theology about a different kind of power. Not the power of control or the power of being over or being under, but the power of fertility . . . the creative energy of God."

The Navajo people have a rite called the *blessingway*. Performed at the important crossroads of life, the blessingway addresses the great questions and offers a path of holiness. It is a path to happiness, peace, and plenty. Blessingway songs, the basis of the Navajo ceremonial structure, portray how those in a state of blessing relate to one another.

Every culture has its own expressions of blessing and offers ways to live in community and abundance. There are many ways to offer blessing to others. One way is to place your hand on the head or shoulders of a loved one and offer a prayer for healing and guidance. Christians lay hands on people and anoint them with oil, praying for God's blessing and help. To say grace before a meal offers thanks not only to the God who provides, but perhaps even to the food itself, as in some Native hunting cultures.

Another approach to blessing is to bless others without words, sending thoughts of peace and wellness to strangers and to all the people we encounter in our everyday life. Wish them well in every circumstance. Though your first reaction may be to curse the person who cuts you off in traffic, I recommend the quiet choice—to bless and pray for them. Silently say a simple prayer, "May you be happy. May you be at peace." Say it not only to people, but also to animals and to all of life. Make it a prayer that comes from the deep center of your heart.

Affirmations can also be blessings. Make positive statements that proclaim blessing, well-being, and thanksgiving. Reading aloud sacred scriptures from your spiritual tradition can be a way of blessing. Being aware of the gifts of life and thanking the Giver for the many blessings of each day is a path to more blessing.

Creating a home that is a sanctuary of peace and beauty, running a business that balances profitability with the needs of workers and customers, growing food to sustain others—every daily endeavor, from driving a truck to stocking store shelves, can be an expression of blessing when done with the right attitude.

Art, music, and creative endeavors bring blessing into the world. Teaching children, making crafts, tending the sick, cooking meals, cleaning the house, doing your work honestly, treating others kindly—all these activities can be signs of grace and a humble blessing, when we put our hearts into them.

Blessings are extended through service to others. There are many opportunities for volunteering your time and sharing yourself with others. Anything from a simple smile to an afternoon at the local women's shelter, hospice, or food bank, can create a circle of giving to pass the blessings on. To offer your life—your time, energy, and resources—is a gift that will sow many blessings in your life and in the lives of others.

It is also a blessing for you to be involved with important issues of our day. If you are concerned about the environmental crisis, the rights of those who have no champions, the spiritual and physical needs of those who don't have enough, or political and social injustices that need to be addressed, you have a special gift to offer the world through your involvement. Though our age is a cynical one, we need idealists who are willing to take on the system and make a stand for what they truly believe.

The Northwest Native culture has a tradition of *potlatch*, which is a ceremonial act of giving away wealth in order to gain social respect. In a society that knows the price of everything and the value of nothing, perhaps we could learn from a society in which people gained value by giving things away, rather than measuring a person's worth by the size of their bank account. For the Haida people of the Pacific Coast, the road to greatness was not through conquest or accumulation, but through great potlatches. Perhaps we can find new definitions of value and create a more just, generous, and blessed way of life. What can you do to bless others and to be a blessing today?

*I learned that simply to ask a blessing upon one's circumstances,
whatever they are, is somehow to improve them, and to tap some
mysterious source of energy and joy. I came upon one of the most ancient and
universal truths—that to affirm and claim God's help even before
it is given, is to receive it.*

—MARJORIE HOLMES

The Lord bless thee,
and keep thee:
The Lord make his face shine upon thee,
and be gracious unto thee:
The Lord lift up his countenance upon thee,
and give thee peace.
—NUMBERS 6:24–26 (KJV)

What do we live for if not to make life less difficult for each other?
—GEORGE ELIOT

If we live good lives, the times are also good. As we are, such are the times.
—SAINT AUGUSTINE

A kind word is like a spring day.
—RUSSIAN PROVERB

An unshared life is not living. He who shares
does not lessen, but greatens, his life.
—STEPHEN S. WISE

Behold! I do not give lectures on a little charity. When I give, I give myself.

—WALT WHITMAN

If you judge people, you have no time to love them.

—MOTHER TERESA

Judge not, that you be not judged.
For with the judgement you pronounce you will be judged,
and the measure you give will be the measure you get.

—MATTHEW 7:1–2 (RSV)

Great Spirit, help me never to judge another
until I have walked two weeks in his moccasins.

—LAKOTA PRAYER

People are lonely because they build walls instead of bridges.

—JOSEPH FORT NEWTON

Help your brother's boat across, and your own will reach the shore.

—HINDU PROVERB

Man's ultimate aim is the realization of God,
and all his activities—social, political, religious—
have to be guided by the ultimate aim of the vision of God.
The immediate service of all human beings becomes a
necessary part of the endeavour, simply because the only way
to find God is to see him in his creation and be one with it.
This can only be done by service of all.

—MAHATMA GANDHI

We can reject everything else: religion, ideology,
all received wisdom. But we cannot escape
the necessity of love and compassion.

—THE DALAI LAMA

Any religion which professes to be concerned
about the souls of men and is not concerned about
the social and economic conditions that can scar the soul,
is a spiritually moribund religion only waiting for the day to be buried.

—MARTIN LUTHER KING, JR.

The presence of God is felt not only when you shut your eyes;
God can also be seen when one looks around.
Service to the hungry, poor, sick, and ignorant,
in the proper spirit, is as effective as any other spiritual discipline.
—RAMAKRISHNA PARAMAHASA

Come, O blessed of my Father, inherit the kingdom prepared for you
from the foundation of the world; for I was hungry and you gave me food,
I was thirsty and you gave me drink, I was a stranger and you welcomed me,
I was naked and you clothed me, I was sick and you visited me, I was in
prison and you came to me. . . . Truly, I say to you, as you did it to one of the
least of these my brethren, you did it to me.
—MATTHEW 25:34–36, 40 (RSV)

SEEING BEYOND THE SHADOWS

Our task must be to widen our circle of compassion,
to embrace all living creatures and the whole of nature in its beauty.

—ALBERT EINSTEIN

How do you view your world? Do you see it through a media lens of cynicism and fragmentation? Or do you look with your own eyes for the connections and beauty in life? The media, corporations, and power structures of our society are focused on turning you into a passive consumer whose thoughts can be controlled, appetites stimulated, and dreams suppressed.

Look at those slickly produced advertisements. Do you have the eyes to see beyond the images to the truth in your own heart? Look at the skinny models—male and female—with unhappy faces and slouched poses. This is not the sweet, slender insouciance of Audrey Hepburn in the fifties or the wide-eyed awkwardness of Twiggy in the sixties. This is a studied effort to reduce men and women (and especially adolescent girls) to a mere shadow of their potential fullness.

Some photographers, fashion designers, and graphic artists even brag that they create images of ugly hopelessness on purpose—a trendier-than-thou subculture of people who are dying of eternal hipness. These creative people are proud of the fact that they draw inspiration from the drug culture. It's one way to feed the addictive consumer culture of our society. Is it social statement or callous manipulation? Only you can decide.

> *Every time we walk down the street,*
> *we are preceded by a host of angels singing,*
> *"Make way, make way, make way for the image of God."*
> —RABBINIC SAYING

I'm a baby boomer who grew up with Barbie, Ken, and all the other fashion dolls. Those elongated figures with exaggerated body shapes defined a certain form for fashion, much as the wasp-waisted, cruelly corseted figures of another era squeezed women's bodies into a doll-like mold that had no relation to the needs of living, breathing flesh. Today's media darlings all seem to be coming from a similar mold—teenage blondes singing sexy songs and baring their boobs and booties to sell records. Stiff-muscled young men stretch out on the magazine page like beef displayed in a butcher's window.

Cheesecake and beefcake—the fast-food intimacy of artificial images is selling us into slavery to an unrealistic worldview that parodies the power and passion of life.

Fashion can be fun, and each generation has its own tastes. The joys of the fashion statement, the frivolity and fluff of media heroes and heroines, and the slick images of modern life all have their place. But they should not define who we are or what we aspire to become. Slick images are no substitute for the real world in all its messy glory. Teenage girls should not feel it's necessary to starve themselves to achieve a body natural to only a small proportion of the population. Nor should the pressure to look a certain way encourage young men to take dangerous steroids to achieve a superhero's muscled torso. If we can perceive value only in the limited media vision of perfection, we will miss all the fascinating and complex wonder of the real world we inhabit.

I have declared a one-woman revolt. I am choosing to focus on images of beauty, grace, and fullness. Instead of slick fashion magazines that are here today and gone tomorrow, I look at timeless art. I especially love the Impressionists, as they enable me to see the beauty of my own body type.

An artist friend once told me that I reminded her of a Renoir painting, and I have adopted this image for myself. No longer a short, round failure because I wasn't born with a long torso and slender legs, I visualize myself as a warm-hearted, life-embracing, Renoir party girl. My round face and soft, feminine shape have much more in common with the rosy-lipped maidens of the artist's parties on the Seine than some photo of a bored, skinny model pouting at me from a fashion page.

Are there painted worlds—images of other times and other places—that can teach us to see beyond the limitations of our current culture? Can those images give our imaginations a more colorful palette from which to create our own images? Can the values of a Renaissance painter, a Greek sculptor, or an ancient Egyptian stone-carver help us weigh and measure our own values and our own time?

Do we dare look at each other as members of a community instead of as individuals in competition? Do we hunger for something more when we look at images of unfenced prairie, of deep primeval forests uncut forever, of villages surrounded by natural beauty, of the simple gifts of life in bread and cheese and fruit? Paintings give us clues to the beauties that life can hold, uncluttered by long freeway commutes, plastic packaging, landfills, smokestacks, exhaust fumes, and urban sprawl. They remind us that gardens and growing things, well-designed buildings set like jewels in a natural landscape, and time for relaxing with friends bring a feeling of gracious plenty to life. These are the pictures to contemplate if we wish to visualize a better world.

Cynics will say that such idealism is naïve, that we must be "real" and understand that "time is money," and that there is no going back to a simpler time and place. I know there was no Golden Age. And I know that the rustic peasants enjoying their simple bread and fruit did not have antibiotics or the opportunities our modern society offers us. But why not choose to take the best from both worlds?

I am no longer convinced that the assumptions of our modern culture are necessarily the correct view of what life can and should be. I now question the reductionist, materialistic worldview that assumes that money is the measure of all things and that everything must be sacrificed to achieve economic growth. The tools now used for measuring economic growth measure only money—not compassion, sustainability, or the human cost of worshipping the bottom line.

I believe we can create a quiet revolution, one person at a time, by daring to question the unspoken assumptions of the mass culture. I believe we can begin by dreaming of new images of beauty, community, and meaning. We start with how we perceive ourselves, then how we perceive others, and finally how we perceive our planet. What images do you choose to define your present reality and your dreams for the future?

The theoretical intelligence merely contemplates the world, and the practical intelligence merely orders it; but the aesthetic intelligence creates the world.
—FRIEDRICH SCHELLING

Politics have a very close affinity to art.
—SIMONE WEIL

Our art must be the foundation of the coming culture.
—KENJI MIYAZAWA

Imagination is the secret marrow of civilization.
It is the very eye of faith.
—HENRY WARD BEECHER

If you ask me what I came to do in this world,
I, an artist, will answer you: I am here to live out loud.
—EMILE ZOLA

He knows himself greatly who never opposes his greatness.
—WILLIAM BLAKE

Before a painter puts a brush to his canvas
he sees his picture mentally. If you think of yourself in terms
of a painting, what do you see? Is the picture one you
think worth painting? You create yourself in the
image you hold in your mind.

—THOMAS DREIER

And God saw everything that he had made,
and behold, it was very good.

—GENESIS 1:31 (RSV)

Nothing befalls us that is not of the nature of ourselves. There comes no adventure
but wears to our soul the shape of our everyday thoughts.

—MAURICE MAETERLINCK

Change your thoughts and you change your world.

—NORMAN VINCENT PEALE

*Every totalitarian regime is frightened of the artist.
It is the vocation of the prophet to keep alive the ministry of
the imagination, to keep on conjuring and proposing
alternative futures to the single one the
king wants to urge as the only thinkable one.*

—WALTER BREUGGEMANN

*By consigning away our power and confining ourselves in consumerism's gilded
cage, we lose the ability to actively choose the shape of our communities.*

—THOMAS PRUGH

Pay attention to what they tell you to forget.

—MURIEL RUKEYSER

*The function of art is to do more than tell it like it is—
it's to imagine what's possible.*

—BELL HOOKS

In the beginner's mind, there are many possibilities. In the expert's, there are few.

—SHINRYU SUZUKI

Not to dream more boldly may turn out to be,
in view of present realities, simply irresponsible.
—GEORGE LEONARD

We don't see things as they are, we see them as we are.
—ANAÏS NIN

Our deepest fear is not that we are inadequate.
Our deepest fear is that we are powerful beyond measure.
—MARIANNE WILLIAMSON

Belief conditions experience, and experience
then strengthens belief. What you believe, you experience.
—JIDDU KRISHNAMURTI

Let the words of my mouth and the meditation of my heart
be acceptable in thy sight, O Lord, my rock and my redeemer.
—PSALM 19:14 (RSV)

The creation of a thousand forests is in one acorn.

—RALPH WALDO EMERSON

Take only what you need and leave the land as you found it.

—ARAPAHO PROVERB

In a real sense all life is interrelated. All are caught in an inescapable network of mutuality, tied in a single garment of destiny.

—MARTIN LUTHER KING, JR.

Whenever a person breaks a stick in the forest, let him consider what it would feel like if it were himself that was thus broken.

—NIGERIAN PROVERB

Be kind to everything that lives.

—OMAHA PROVERB

O Lord, how manifold are thy works! In wisdom thou hast made them all; the earth is full of thy creatures.

—PSALM 104:24 (RSV)

The earth was placed here for us . . .
and we consider her our Mother.
How much would you ask for
if your Mother had been harmed?
No amount of money can repay.
Money cannot give birth to anything.

—ASA BAZHONOODAH, NAVAJO WRITER

This world, this palpable world, which we are wont to treat with the boredom and
disrespect with which we habitually regard places with no sacred association for
us, is in truth a holy place, and we did not know it. Venite adoremus.

—PIERRE TEILHARD DE CHARDIN

Whoever possesses God in their being has him in a divine manner,
and he shines out to them in all things; for them all things taste of God and
in all things it is God's image they see.

—MEISTER ECKHART

The fullness of joy is to behold God in everything.

—JULIAN OF NORWICH

The Art of Encouragement

To love is to transform; to be a poet.

—NORMAN O. BROWN

ENCOURAGEMENT

*Life is short and we have not too much time for gladdening the
hearts of those who are traveling the dark way with us.
Oh, be swift to love! Make haste to be kind!*
—HENRI F. AMIEL

Encouragement . . .
is not lecturing people about what they should do or what they
should be, but holding up a positive mirror and showing them what
they already are or have the potential to become.

Encouragement . . .
"believes all things, hopes all things, endures all things" because of love.

Encouragement . . .
comes from one fellow traveler to another fellow traveler—
we are all in this together.

The Art of Encouragement

Encouragement . . .
critiques but never criticizes, and is always willing to look for the good.

Encouragement . . .
is the art of helping people discover their own beauty,
potential, and uniqueness.

Encouragement . . .
is the joy of sharing the load for a small portion of the journey.

Encouragement . . .
is someone to laugh with, to cry with, to rejoice with in happiness
and share with in sorrow.

Encouragement . . .
is a lamp in the window on a dark and stormy night.

Encouragement . . .
is a smile and a helping hand.

I'm going your way, so let us go hand in hand.
You help me and I'll help you.
We shall not be here for very long, for soon death,
the kind old nurse, will come back and rock us all to sleep.
Let us help one another while we may.

—WILLIAM MORRIS

And behold, a woman of the city, when she learned that he was sitting at table in
the Pharisee's house, brought an alabaster flask of ointment, and standing behind
him at his feet, weeping, she began to wet his feet with her tears, and wiped them
with the hair of her head, and kissed his feet, and anointed them with oil.

—LUKE 7:37-38 (RSV)

Do not keep the alabaster boxes of your love and
tenderness sealed up until your friends are dead.
Fill their lives with sweetness. Speak approving,
cheering words while their ears can hear them and
while their hearts can be thrilled by them.

—HENRY WARD BEECHER

LISTEN AGAIN

Deep calls to deep
at the thunder of thy cataracts;
all thy waves and thy billows
have gone over me.
By day the Lord commands his steadfast love;
and at night his song is with me,
a prayer to the God of my life.
—PSALM 42:7–8 (RSV)

Our society is obsessed with diagnosing "the problem." But the problem may be falsely defined. Are you defining yourself by what's wrong with you? Are you defining your world by how it falls short of your expectations? Are you so busy "fixing" a relationship that you can't see the essential goodness of the person right in front of you?

We tell ourselves stories, and our stories help us make sense of the world. If our story is one of overcoming addiction, of problems in need of solution, or about how we are misunderstood artists, tortured by gifts the world doesn't want—is this the only story we have to tell? If we define and defend and defeat our problem, are we not then able to move beyond the problem into a new story, another experience? The once-addicted author who was almost suicidal—can she tell the story of overcoming addiction, but also plunge into a fresh, new expansion of her gifts and personality, now that she's freed from her dependence on pill or bottle? When the marriage is off the rocks and on an even keel again, is the couple willing to brave the next new adventure?

When we finish school, we graduate and move on to the wider world. But we never stop learning. Sometimes we can be like believers who are so obsessed with an initial conversion experience, they forget that they were saved to live a new life. We sometimes miss the point that we are bigger than our diagnosis, greater than some problem confronted and solved. Diagnosis and treatment are only part of the journey of our lives, and are meant to free us to *live* our lives.

Once we are saved, what work and adventure are now available to us in our newfound freedom? And if we are called to a greater work, how much more reason there is to seek help and discover solutions and cures in the first place. We know we are not meant to be stuck in the hospital of life forever, but are called to express the beauty, goodness, and truth of our lives in ever new, ever expanding realms. Even death itself may be seen as a great adventure—an unknown on the other side of the grave for us to explore.

Listen, and you will hear the sounds of life, the heartbeat of the cosmos. Turn down the noise, the clamor of voices shouting at you; trying to persuade you; telling you what to believe, what is good for you, what you need to buy, whom you need to impress, what things are essential to your well-being. All these voices—from the television and radio and newspaper and society and job—want to define you and put you in a box with a label on it, neat and tidy, ordered and controllable. Shutting off those yelling, yammering voices and allowing the silence to wash over you is not only a healing choice, it is an empowering choice. By choosing to spend some time in silence and meditation, you are taking back your life.

In the silence, you will find that, like Jacob, you are wrestling with an angel. It is an angel that reveals your weakness—and your strength. You can no longer avoid your fears or shield your ears with the noise and agendas of others. You can no longer make excuses. You can no longer hide from your own potential, either. It is time to listen to the cry of your soul and to let the tears flow. Your greatest fears hide your greatest treasures.

And, as you wrestle with angels and demons, as you allow your soul the breathing space to listen, soon you will hear a still, small voice. It is the voice of the heart, that says you are more whole than you knew, larger than you imagined. You are far more than the limited definitions you have lived by for so many years. Your problems no longer define who you are—they are just lessons for you to learn. You are a child of hope and wonder, beloved by God and created to offer a unique and irreplaceable gift to this world. You are valuable just because you are alive. In your deepest heart, you contact this beautiful awareness that you are whole, magical, beloved, and helped by the universe in ways you have yet to understand.

This listening goes deep into the pure heart you once knew in childhood. Then you looked at everything with eyes of wonder. Now you are becoming like a child once more, with the dawning awareness that the kingdom of Heaven has been within you all along. Heaven has always been with you, no matter how obscured by the flotsam and jetsam of life's storms and crises and problems. Deep, deep, deep under the waves lie the still, dark depths of the heart of the ocean—your spirit, rediscovered in the silence.

And when you surface again, as you come up out of the stillness and silence to re-enter your life, you discover that when you encounter another human heart, deep calls to deep. Because you have recovered the treasures of the wonder and sacredness of your own being, you are now able to see and hear and feel the sacredness and wonder of other human beings. You know how to listen past the surface and go beneath to hear the true heart speak.

Once you have tasted the listening, you return again and again to the stillness. You return to hear the voice of your heart and to be empowered to hear the voice of all hearts, beating in time to the hidden rhythms of the cosmos. Listen. Do you hear the sound of God's heart beating?

I do not know what I may appear to the world; but to myself I seem to have been only like a boy playing on the seashore, and diverting myself in now and then finding a smoother pebble or a prettier shell than ordinary, whilst the great ocean of truth lay all undiscovered before me.

—ISAAC NEWTON

Silence is the garden of meditation.

—ALI

You wish to see; Listen. Hearing is a step toward Vision.

—SAINT BERNARD OF CLAIRVAUX

For the Great Spirit is everywhere; he hears whatever is in our minds and hearts,
and it is not necessary to speak to him in a loud voice.
—BLACK ELK

Speak Lord; for thy servant heareth.
—I SAMUEL 3:9 (KJV)

Be still and cool in thy own mind and spirit.
—GEORGE FOX

Never say there is nothing beautiful in the world anymore. There is always
something to make you wonder, in the shape of a leaf, the trembling of a tree.
—ALBERT SCHWEITZER

The mystery of life is not a problem to be solved, it is a reality to be lived.
—AART VAN DER LEEUWARDEN

Numberless are the world's wonders, but none more wonderful than man.
—SOPHOCLES

So God created man in his own image, in the image of God he created him;
male and female he created them.

—GENESIS 1:27 (RSV)

The most beautiful thing we can experience is the mysterious.
It is the source of all true art and all science.
He to whom this emotion is a stranger, who can no longer
pause to wonder and stand rapt in awe,
is as good as dead; his eyes are closed.

—ALBERT EINSTEIN

If you see in any given situation only what everybody
else can see, you can be said to be so much a representative of
your culture that you are a victim of it.

—S. I. HAYAKAWA

Every man takes the limits of his field of vision
for the limits of the world.

—ARTUR SCHOPENHAUER

Compared to what we ought to be, we are half awake.
—WILLIAM JAMES

The great man is he who does not lose his child's heart.
—MENCIUS

Your own mind is a sacred enclosure into which
nothing harmful can enter except by your permission.
—ARNOLD BENNETT

No work of love will flourish out of guilt, fear,
or hollowness of heart, just as no valid plans for the future
can be made by those who have no capacity for living now.
—ALAN WATTS

I think that what we're seeking is an experience of being alive,
so that our life experiences on the purely physical plane
will have resonances within our innermost being and reality,
so that we actually feel the rapture of being alive.
—JOSEPH CAMPBELL

A musician must make his music, an artist must paint,
a poet must write if he is to ultimately be at peace with himself.

—ABRAHAM MASLOW

In our whole life melody the music is broken off here and there by rests, and
we foolishly think we have come to the end of time. God sends a time of forced
leisure, a time of sickness and disappointed plans, and makes a sudden pause in
the hymn of our lives, and we lament that our voice must be silent and our part
missing in the music which ever goes up to the ear of our Creator. Not without
design does God write the music of our lives. Be it ours to learn the time and not be
dismayed at the rests. If we look up, God will beat the time for us.

—JOHN RUSKIN

He that hath ears to hear, let him hear.

—MATTHEW 11:15 (KJV)

All are but parts of one stupendous whole,
Whose body nature is, and God the soul.

—ALEXANDER POPE

Marvelous power,

marvelous action!

Chopping wood,

carrying water…

—CHINESE ZEN MASTER'S SAYING

Before enlightenment, I chopped wood and carried water; after

enlightenment, I chopped wood and carried water.

—ZEN SAYING

THE VOICE OF THE HEART

The art of living rightly is like all arts; it must be learned
and practiced with incessant care.

—GOETHE

When you listen to your heart, you will hear a voice of clarity and hope . . .
Don't be halfway. Embrace your life as it is. Make it what you want it to be. Be proactive. Be positive. Cultivate a savvy optimism. Don't listen to the pessimists. Dare to dream. Dare to dream your fondest, sweetest, richest dreams—those nearest and dearest to your heart. Do not be halfhearted. Don't make halfway mistakes—just give yourself permission to stumble, then do whatever you choose to do, with your whole heart.

Don't try to love with half a heart—you could live your whole life half hearted, halfway. If you are going to love someone, you must love them with your whole heart, with every fiber of your being. Stop weighing and measuring others, looking for perfection. There is no such thing as perfection in people. But there is a perfection of love that transcends the differences and problems. Love with all your heart.

Give generously. Don't hold back. Speak your love aloud, show your feelings, even if you risk acting like a fool. Be openhearted—do not judge yourself or others. Your feelings are real and do not lie. But we lie to ourselves when we try to deny our true heart's emotions. Do not be ashamed of your feelings—acknowledge them. Learn to listen to what they tell you. Learn to move beyond the negatives and to enhance the positives. Always be willing to risk yourself. Love generously, with feeling and passion.

Make each day wonderful in its own way. Instead of wishing for what you don't have, look at what is available to you. How much do you choose to embrace in your own life? Whom do you choose to embrace in love? What risks do you take? How many new things are you willing to try? How many tiny steps of faith are you willing to take? How do you go about embracing your community and the opportunities and needs that come with this particular place and time and situation?

We always attract into our lives whatever we think about most,
believe in most strongly, expect on the deepest level, and imagine most vividly.
—SHAKTI GAWAIN

Work from your heart. Throw yourself into good work. Be creative. Aim high and work for the highest good. Choose deep, satisfying work that allows you to nurture your gifts and express your true self. Let your work expand and fill the empty spaces in your life. Know that your heartfelt work is a bridge into the life you want—*is* the life you want. Put the weight of your longing into heartfelt work and let the work lead you to unexpected delights and new destinations. Allow worthy, heartfelt work to become your process of healing and growth.

Do not close yourself off from life because of fear. Do not build walls of expectations or dictate terms for who, what, how, and when the Universe will deliver. Expect miracles and see miracles, even in the simple, mundane round of life. Love each moment as it comes. Embrace it fully. Immerse yourself in *this* moment, *this* reality. Be aware. Be yourself. Be brave and dare to live from the very center of your being.

Adventure can be an end in itself. Self-discovery is the secret
ingredient that fuels daring.
—GRACE LICHTENSTEIN

When you have a choice between following your heart or following your head, always listen to your heart first. Know that you are not alone. The still, small voice speaks when you are willing to listen. You are surrounded by the love of the Universe; you are guided by God; you are ministered to by His angels, watched over by saints and ancestors. Embrace your life today. Live in the music and dance to the rhythm of love. Dare to live with your whole heart, every single day of your life.

Alas for those who never sing, but die with all their music in them.
—OLIVER WENDELL HOLMES

When one does not love too much, one does not love enough.
—BLAISE PASCAL

Dare to be naïve.
—R. BUCKMINSTER FULLER

The only real security is not insurance or money or a job, not a house and furniture paid for, or a retirement fund, and never is it another person. It is the skill and humor and courage within, the ability to build your own fires and find your own peace.

—AUDREY SUTHERLAND

People generally think that it is the world, the environment, external relationships, which stand in one's way, in the way of one's good fortune. . . . and at the bottom is always man himself that stands in his own way.

—SØREN KIERKEGAARD

Life begets life. Energy creates energy. It is by spending oneself that one becomes rich.

—SARAH BERNHARDT

Yesterday I dared to struggle. Today I dare to win.

—BERNADETTE DEVLIN

You are not living by human laws but by divine laws. Expect miracles and see them take place. Hold ever before you the thought of prosperity and abundance, and know that doing so sets in motion forces that will bring it into being.

—EILEEN CADDY

No one has ever seen God. Yet if we love one another God dwells in us, and his love is brought to perfection in us.

—I JOHN 4:12 (NAB)

It is not who you are or what you have been that God sees with His all-merciful eyes, but what you desire to be.

—*THE CLOUD OF UNKNOWING*

There is no going alone on a journey.
Whether one explores strange lands or Main Street or
one's own backyard, always invisible traveling companions
are close by: the giants and pygmies of memory, of belief,
pulling you this way and that, not letting you see the world
life-size but insisting that you measure it by
their own height and weight.

—LILLIAN SMITH

Oh! May the God of green hope fill you up with joy, fill you up
with peace, so that your believing lives, filled with the life-giving energy of the
Holy Spirit, will brim over with hope!

—ROMANS 15:13 (THE MESSAGE)

O God, who hast prepared for those who love thee
such good things as pass understanding:
Pour into our hearts such love toward thee, that we,
loving thee in all things and above all things,
may obtain thy promises, which exceed all that we can desire.
—*THE BOOK OF COMMON PRAYER*

Benediction

Go on your way in peace.

Be of good courage.

Hold fast that which is good.

Render to no man evil for evil.

Strengthen the fainthearted.

Support the weak.

Help and cheer the sick.

Honor all men.

Love and serve the Lord.

May the blessing of God be upon you and remain with you forever.

Amen

—FROM GLOUCESTER CATHEDRAL

221

About the Author

Candy Paull is the author of *The Art of Simplicity*, *The Art of Abundance*, *The Art of Encouragement*, and *Christmas Abundance*. A performing singer/songwriter, Candy has been a freelance writer specializing in marketing materials for book publishers, as well as being a buyer for bookstores and a marketing director for a small publisher.

Candy's open approach to spirituality draws insight and wisdom from many spiritual traditions, emphasizing that there is something within us that is trustworthy, whole, and wise. Instead of always trying to "fix" what is "broken" in our lives, she helps us experience the profound wholeness that lies at the center of the universe—and in our own human hearts. Through words and music, she takes complex concepts like grace, truth, goodness, beauty, sacredness, holiness, love, and mercy, and translates them into quiet wisdom that nourishes and enriches daily life.

Candy speaks, sings, and facilitates retreats that combine movement, music, readings, aromatherapy, and other healing modalities to help men and women reduce stress, enjoy a more creative and abundant life, and nurture spiritual growth by integrating body, mind, and spirit. She also speaks at conferences, seminars, and corporate events.

Candy Paull
P.O. Box 159276
Nashville, TN 37215
www.candypaull.com

Candy would like to thank Stephany Evans, Marisa Bulzone, Frank DeMarco, Donna Michael, Gerrie McDowell, Loretta Barrett, Arnold Gosewich, Sue Sumeraj, and Gillian Watts for their help and encouragement in the creation of this book.

Credits